See page 80 !
Best wishes
Tony

The author, 1980

About
Twenty Five Years
of Cricket

A History of
Reading University Academic Staff
Cricket Club

Written & Edited by Tony Giles
1983

Published by RUASCC 1983

ISBN 0 7049 0499 3

Designed and printed in the
Department of Typography & Graphic Communication
University of Reading

Contents

Acknowledgements

Many people have helped to compile this history. In the first place, eleven playing members (David Ansell, Mike Butler, Peter Crane, Joe Gartner, Roger Loader, David Petherick, Bob Pearce, Richard Tranter, Mike Sewell, Mike Pursglove and Mike Biddiss) between them analysed the averages and playing record for the seasons 1964-82. Four of them (Richard Tranter, Mike Sewell, Mike Pursglove and Jim Knowlson) have subsequently helped enormously in checking typescript and final proofs. Finally, amongst the players, Mike Sewell helped to prepare some of the career records that appear towards the end of the book, and was entirely responsible for devising the idea of the 'Gallery of Sporting Prints' to which, subsequently, numerous players contributed ideas. Who, precisely, suggested what, will remain my secret!

We are especially grateful to Mrs Lorna Turner who not only typed most of the text, but with a minimum of editorial guidance, carefully converted a wide variety of manuscripts and initial typings into a uniform presentation. We are also grateful to Jean Robertson, Keith Hodgson and Ted Bell in the Registrar's Office, and Tom Keeley and Cliff Morris in the Department of Typography & Graphic Communication for guidance and assistance at the production end of things. The photographs have been taken by various members of the University's photographic staff, by Peter Hotten and by Peter Keel of Leighton Park School.

Finally, no documented history would have been possible if score books had not been completed and our thanks to those who, over the years, have done that particular chore, are recorded in the text. The fact, however, that score books have been used as the main source for this history means that full details of each player's initials, and his Department, have not always been available. Every attempt has been made to obtain those details but in some cases, especially where students or others have 'guested' for RUASCC such details remain incomplete. This is no reflection, of course, on the scorers who do well at the time if they get the surnames right — but we offer our apologies to those concerned.

Tony Giles

Captains, Vice-Captains and Honorary Life Members

	Captain	Vice Captain
1957 to		
1962	F. Robertson	None
1963	S. Fox	None
1964	A. Harrison	A. K. Giles
1965	A. K. Giles	W. D. Redfern
1966	W. D. Redfern	B. Loughbrough
1967	A. Harrison	R. W. Willey
1968	R. W. Willey	D. H. Robertson
1969	R. W. Willey	M. J. Sewell
1970	A. K. Giles	D. J. Ansell
1971	A. K. Giles	D. J. Ansell
1972	D. J. Ansell	G. E. Dalton
1973	D. J. Ansell	G. E. Dalton
1974	D. J. Ansell	G. E. Dalton
1975	D. J. Ansell	G. E. Dalton
1976	J. R. Knowlson	A. K. Giles
1977	J. R. Knowlson	A. K. Giles
1978	M. J. Sewell	A. K. Giles
1979	M. J. Sewell	R. B. Tranter
1980	M. J. Sewell	R. B. Tranter
1981	M. J. Sewell	R. B. Tranter & D. M. Pursglove
1982	D. J. Ansell	R. B. Tranter & D. M. Pursglove

Honorary Life Members

A. Harrison (1971)
F. Robertson (1971)
K. Robinson (1977)

6

List of Players – by Department 1964–1982

Despite extensive research, the considerable number of members of staff, students and guests who have played very occasionally to help make up sides (especially in the early days of the Club), and whose initials and Department have not been recorded in the score books, means that the following list cannot be claimed to be complete. It is believed, however, that it contains the names of all those members of staff, postgraduates and research assistants who have played at all regularly between the years specified. Some others who played before 1964 are mentioned in the short history. The Departments (using their present-day titles) are listed in alphabetical order, and within each Department, players are listed in the order in which they first played for the Club.

Agriculture & Horticulture
S. Fox
R. Barnwell
R. W. Willey
J. B. Dent
P. M. Harris
G. E. Dalton
M. R. Heslehurst
C. R. C. Hendy
D. Griffis
M. D. S. Butler
D. J. Petherick
J. A. Gartner
G. Lee
L. Prevost

Agricultural Economics & Management
A. Harrison
A. K. Giles
G. A. Urquhart
D. J. Ansell
C. Ritson
T. E. Josling
M. Hallam
D. Crush

Applied Statistics
R. Meade
R. D. Stern

Botany
D. Robeson
P. R. Crane
S. W. Adkins
M. Owen
G. E. Whitelam
C. Miles

Bursar's Office
J. A. Ford

Centre for Agricultural Strategy
R. B. Tranter
A. Thompson

Chaplaincy Centre
A. Smithson

Chemistry
J. M. Hollas
A. G. Robiette
D. E. Penny
D. J. Smith
A. J. Benton
J. S. Elder
T. Ridley
D. Williams
J. Budd
I. Warburton
M. Lewis

Computer Science
R. J. Loader

Classics
F. Robertson

Construction Management
N. A. D. Morrison

Economics
D. R. Thomas
M. A. Utton
D. H. Robertson
R. D. Pearce

8

Economics continued
F. Stilwell
C. Hemmings
G. R. Crampton
A. R. Rugman
A. Fisher
G. Norman
K. Patterson

Education
P. Oakley
N. Stockton

Engineering
A. J. Pretlove
H. S. Dobbs

English
J. R. Lucas
I. Fletcher

Food Science
R. W. Ison

French Studies
W. D. Redfern
J. E. Flower
J. R. Knowlson

Geography
R. Tiwari
D. H. S. Foot
D. Russell
D. J. Bannister
D. G. Hay
A. Amin
S. Flemming
J. R. Short
D. Donkin

Geology
J. E. Thomas
R. MacDonald
P. Wright

German
M. Mitchell
J. P. Wieczorek

Grounds Staff
F. G. Stokes
J. Smith

History
C. W. Chalklin
M. D. Biddiss
F. Tallett

History of Art
P. Fitzgerald

**Land Management &
Development**
D. Edwards
A. E. Baum
B. Curtis
M. R. Avis
I. Thomson

Mathematics
I. P. Williams
J. K. Dugdale
M. J. Baines
M. J. Sewell
B. D. Dore

Meteorology
B. J. Hoskins
A. Seraphin

9

Microbiology
P. M. Hotten
P. Berry

Museum of English Rural Life
B. Loughbrough
E. J. T. Collins

Physics
K. Robinson
B. L. Evans
S. D. Smith
C. R. Pidgeon
M. J. Sangster

Physiology & Biochemistry
C. H. Walker
G. M. H. Waites
M. I. Mackness
C. Jones
M. Edwards

Politics
K. R. Gladdish
P. A. Allum
P. J. Giddings

Russian
D. M. Pursglove

St Patrick's Hall
F. H. Anderson

Zoology
K. Simkiss
A. R. Jones
A. Orme

Regular Guests
M. Petrie
T. Walden

10

A short history of the club

The Origins

There is one incident in the life of the Club which, perhaps
more than any other, captures the spirit with which its cricket
has been approached. It happened in 1972. David Ansell, in
the first of his four years as captain, felt it would be helpful if
the Club joined the Club Cricket Conference. Apart from any
other advantages, this would assist in finding opponents at
short notice if fixtures were cancelled. The C. C. C.'s reply
gave rise to some initial embarrassment. As a first condition of
membership, they asked for a copy of the Club's rules — and
there were none! A lengthy discussion at the next AGM,
that would have done credit to any group of academics,
confirmed that not only had the Club gradually come into
existence without any rules at all — but that it was efficiently
run, played and enjoyed a lot of cricket, and that (even at the
cost of not being able to join the Club Cricket Conference) no
rules seemed necessary. This situation still exists today,
although an unwritten set of rules is clearly understood and
within them cricket flourishes, with some fifty matches each
season.

Perhaps it was something of this same desire not to formalise
things too much that, back in the middle 1950s, led those who
were to become the Club's earliest regular players to be
satisfied with net practice, without actually going to the bother
of playing matches! It was sufficient, apparently, for a few
enthusiasts to get together once a week in a net, to the rear of
Whiteknights Hall, before retiring (not too late) to the nearby
'Nob'. Only gradually was this idyllic state — in which nobody
was ever given 'out', nobody dropped a catch that mattered,
and countless unplayable balls were bowled — brought, almost
grudgingly, to an end by allowing opponents to intrude.

11

This hesitant start makes it difficult to say precisely when academic staff cricket in this University began. It depends on how one chooses to define 'staff cricket' and on what constitutes a club. At one extreme it might be argued that, without any rules, RUASCC has no formal existence, even today — although presumably the contents of this book refute that.

At the other extreme, did staff cricket begin — and, therefore, did RUASCC have its first origins — when one member of staff first took an active interest in cricket in the University? The earliest remembered example of this was when Cyril Tyler joined the University from the Royal Agricultural College, Cirencester in 1939. A quick off-spinner who had played regularly for Gloucestershire, and been a contender for even higher honours, Tyler coached the student team, and played for them once in a war-time match at Lord's against the Auxiliary Fire Service. From 1946, until he retired from the game ten years later, Cyril skippered Groundsman 'Sandy' Saunders' XI — a team of mixed talents chosen to play the students. In addition to Cyril Tyler, Sandy's XI usually included, from the academic staff, Deryck Williams and Bob Barnwell — both of whom, like Tyler, were playing for Reading C. C. — Syd Fox and John Prue — the latter once mistaken (on a train!) for Colin Cowdrey. Occasional nets were organised in preparation for these games and some of the same players took part, during the early 1950s, in matches between the Faculty of Agriculture and the National Institute for Research in Dairying.

These players, however, were not to form the regular nucleus of the future academic staff team. Tyler himself decided to hang up his boots in 1956 after the students' opening batsmen — Bob Jones and John Scott — twice within a few weeks (once against Sandy's XI and once against the Old Students XI) scored over 230 for the first wicket. It was not only Cyril Tyler amongst the staff who remembered the occasion ruefully.

12

By this time, however, three more enthusiasts had arrived at the University who were to be important figures in a Club that had yet to be formed: Keith Robinson, Alan Harrison and Fred Robertson. During 1954 and 1955 the previously mentioned habit of regular nets (and retirement to the 'Nob') became well established, and these three players, in their different ways — Keith Robinson mainly with the ball, Alan Harrison mainly with the bat, and Fred Robertson mainly behind the stumps and as an organiser — were to be key members in the earliest academic staff sides. They each enjoyed long playing careers and are now the Club's only Honorary Life Members. Although matches were not to be played until 1957 it was from these regular practice sessions in the middle 1950s that the genuine origins of Reading University Academic Staff Cricket Club can be traced. At the time of writing, it has, therefore, had a life of *about* 25 years — and the rest of this book is *about* them.

Pre-history

Pre-history is the time before records are kept; for RUASCC it was the seven seasons from 1957 until 1963, when matches were played but no score-books were preserved. During the first six of these seven seasons the whole 'outfit' was organised by Fred Robertson, in his customary easy way. There were no elected officers. Fred simply talked Sandy into providing a pitch (no mean task), borrowed some gear, collected together a side, skippered it, kept wicket, and, if necessary, provided the tea. The scores were no doubt kept at the time — but did not survive. Looking back, Fred laughingly confesses that the end of his reign as captain heralded the beginning of proper documentation. He is nearly right, but not quite. Syd Fox followed Fred as the first elected captain in 1963 and had no more enthusiasm for the paper side of cricket than his predecessor.

The very first matches were played in 1957 against the Reading University Employees and the Students 2nd XI. The Employees, organised and captained by Cliff Morris (of Typography) were the cricket section of the Employees Social Club. The Students 2nd XI are still played and are our oldest opponents. Matches, however, were few and far between, due mainly to Sandy's zealous preservation of the 'back wicket' — originally the ladies' pitch with the wicket running parallel to Elmhurst Road.

When the side did play it was 'assembled' rather than 'selected' and (in addition to Robertson, Robinson and Harrison) included, at times, Laurie Carr, John Creed, Norman Barron, Syd Fox, Ian MacPherson, Bill Mitchell, Harry Parkinson, Fred Pickering, John Prue, Tony Smith, Alan Wardman, Len Zatman — strengthened when the students were played by Deryck Williams and Bob Barnwell. This list is probably not complete. Some of those on it were good cricketers and others would hardly claim to be. What they all had in common was that they played a part, without perhaps realising it at the time, in creating a Club that is now thriving. The possibility of over fifty matches a year would have seemed as impossible at the time as a Packer circus!

Two early additions to the fixtures list were to prove stern opponents for some years to come: Ian Fletcher's Particulars and the Academic Staff at Bristol University. The Particulars were a side drawn from cricketers within the University, with a strong flavour of Fletcher's own department, who were not playing for one of the established student or staff sides. Without gear, they were certainly not without talent — notably that of John Lucas — and rivalry between the two sides was always keen.

Then, in 1961, a major step was taken in the direction of reasonably serious club cricket when Bristol University's Academicals Cricket Club — with a well developed fixture list for two sides — asked for a fixture as part of a tour

14

embracing Oxford, Reading and Southampton. The match took place on 7 July. At Bristol's request each side fielded 12 players in order to ensure that everyone in their tour party enjoyed a game. Fred Robertson readily agreed to this request and was able to complete his twelve with Hammond, the current student captain and a strong batsman. Thanks to records kept by Norman Robertson (a Bristol player now in Reading's Faculty of Urban and Regional Studies) we know that the match was drawn after Bristol, batting first, scored 166 for 9 dec. and Reading clung on with 139 for 10. Bristol's twelfth man scored 70 and Hammond was out first ball!

A memorable evening followed and Bristol Academicals, anxious to 'have the opportunity of reciprocating the hospitality', invited RUASCC to Bristol in the following year. It was the Club's first away match, played on the last day of June and was won by Bristol by 5 wickets — RUASCC 107, Bristol Academicals 110 for 5. In the same season RUASCC travelled away to play the Academics C. C. of Southampton University, and received, on tour, the staff C. C. from the University College of South Wales and Monmouthshire. By now the playing strength of the Club had been added to and strengthened. Newer members looking for regular cricket included Brian Evans, Chris Evans, Brian Loughbrough, Tony Giles, Australian Mike Osborne, Des Smith, Wally Redfern, New Zealander Jim Stewart, Roy Thomas, and Iwan Williams. The fixture list for 1963 was extended to ten matches with games against the Wokingham and the Newbury C. C.'s Wednesday XI's added to existing fixtures. RUASCC travelled again to Bristol and were comfortably beaten in a match restricted by rain to 25 overs each, Bristol replying to Reading's 126 for 7 with 130 for 2.

Syd Fox had now become captain and was happy to leave most of the arrangements to Brian Loughbrough, the Club's first secretary. Syd's greatest contribution was his knowledge of the game and firm direction of the side in the field. Alan

15

Harrison still remembers Syd's terse rebuke in the pavilion —
'A draw would have been nice, Alan' — after Alan, the last
recognised batsman, had lost his wicket in his usual search for
quick runs — and the side lost its match against Southampton
Academics. But, along with his firmness, of course Syd
brought great style and humour to the scene both on and off
the field and continued to play occasionally for the Club for
many seasons.

A. G. M.'s, Fixture cards, Score-books and gear

Nobody can quite remember the meeting at which Syd Fox
was appointed captain, but almost certainly there was one,
sparsely attended, and if not held in the Junior Common
Room of Letters Faculty, perhaps in the 'Nob'. There was
certainly a meeting (in the Letters J. C. R.) when Alan Harrison
was elected captain for the 1964 season — although the first
fully minuted A. G. M. did not occur until the morning of
July 10th, 1964. It was recorded that a complete set of gear
had been bought — by Alan Harrison and Tony Giles from the
then Reading School Groundsman, Les Muncer, for a total
cost (including bag) of £37! The author had the pleasure of
being baggageman from then until Peter Crane took over the
job in 1979. Les Muncer remained our supplier for 15 years.
The annual sub was fixed for 1965 at £1, with a match fee of
2/-. For the first time fixture cards were printed, 50 of them
for £1. In the spirit of things at the time it was agreed 'to make
a point of giving as much hospitality as possible to visiting
teams' and Alan Harrison was asked to arrange the Club's first
indoor nets — which he duly did at the Sunningdale Indoor
Cricket School. If this suggested that things were beginning to
be taken seriously, it should be said that any good that was
done at those nets was quickly undone in some lengthy
evenings in the Red Lion, next door. After a few years,

(perhaps with the advent of the breathaliser) indoor nets were moved nearer to home at Alfred Sutton School and more recently still, to Wargrave Piggott and Maiden Erleigh Schools. Each year they mark the approach of a new season; hopes run high; the search for new players is on; the dressing room banter begins afresh — and familiar faults reappear!

From 1964 onwards score books were kept and have been preserved. They provide the main source, along with memory, for the season by season record which takes over from this introductory account of how it all started. Before proceeding to those details however, it seems appropriate to offer some general reflections on the way in which the Club has grown and on some of the people and events which have been important to it.

Reflections

The 1982 fixture card contained fifty-six fixtures. Twenty-five years earlier, as we have seen, those who first represented RUASCC in matches had contented themselves with going through the motions: with nets and with talking cricket in the 'Nob'. After the first few matches in 1957, the fixture list grew slowly but surely, and memory has it that some dozen matches were played under Syd Fox's captaincy in 1963. The growth of fixtures from then on is chronicled in the first table of the 'Club Records' towards the end of the book. The major steps forward came in 1964 (14 games), 1965 (22), 1969 (25), 1974 (29) followed by an almost uninterrupted progression towards the 50 matches that were played in 1982. This growth (which must presumably now come to some sort of halt) has reflected both an increased playing membership and a general change in attitude from the early desire by a few enthusiasts simply to have an occasional game of cricket, to that of an established cricket club with its members looking for all the cricket they can reasonably get. In particular, several of the

17

Club's fixture secretaries — Alan Harrison, David Robertson, Mike Sewell, Mike Butler and David Ansell — had played club cricket elsewhere and brough their enthusiasm for playing and their knowledge of likely opponents to their job.

With the increase in the *amount* of cricket played, there has, naturally, been an increase in the standard of play, not least in the matter of fielding. At its best — as it has been, for instance, when competing for the Sir George Edwards Trophy — there is no doubt that a very good club standard has been reached. The frequent unavailability of key players, however, and the desire in the Club to give cricket to all who show a genuine interest and some modicum of ability, means that our highest playing standards cannot always be maintained. The Club has been fortunate, however, that over the years, the Club's officers have not (except perhaps on those few occasions when the chips are *really* down) allowed playing records to dominate. The less talented players have not only been *selected*, but, as far as possible, have been *'brought into the game'*. The succession of captains — Robertson, Fox, Harrison, Giles, Redfern, Willey, Ansell, Knowlson and Sewell — have all subscribed to that policy. This has not always made the job of captaincy easy, but it would probably be agreed by all concerned that the Club has been fortunate in having captains (and vice-captains) well versed in the game and, more often than not, capable of balancing the needs of the team and the Club with fairness to individuals.

It is often said that cricket is not really a team game and that inevitably the more talented players in any club get more than their share of the action. The achievements of the principal run getters and wicket takers in RUASCC are clearly documented in this history but the presence and contribution of all who have made up an XI on any particular day is fully appreciated. Their presence is, of course, essential and their contribution, often towards the end of an innings or a match, can be crucial. It is precisely in this way that cricket becomes a genuinely team game. The player who bats low down,

18

doesn't bowl and who fields anywhere he is asked to — without complaint — is a priceless asset to any club, and RUASCC is no exception.

But there are no matches, of course, without two teams — and no account of RUASCC would be complete without an expression of appreciation to our opponents: 79 of them between 1964 and 1982. Our record against each of these teams is shown in the 'records' section. In some cases it is good and in others — against Wokingham for instance — it is not so good. But here, it is not the results that we want to emphasise, but the enjoyment and friendships that our opponents have given us. Not all of them can be mentioned individually, but it has given us special pleasure to play against all three XIs of our own students; also to play our opposite numbers in other universities, especially our very long-lasting rivals and friends at Southampton and (until travelling difficulties brought fixtures to an end) at Bristol. Over many years, matches have also been enjoyed, despite the fact that the playing membership of the sides changes each year, with several Service sides, notably the Camberley College Owls and the School of Military Survey at Hermitage, as well as with the Bramshill Police College. With many other clubs, friendships are renewed each year. It is no disrespect to those who are not mentioned if we single out as special rivals and friends over the years: Reading School All Stars, Shiplake College Wanderers, Royal Ascot, Reading Lawyers, Caversham and Leckford.

We have played against too many individuals to begin to mention them, but perhaps two are entitled to a special word. First: John Eggar, when he was Headmaster of Shiplake College. His first-class playing record has been referred to elsewhere in this book, but here we would just like to acknowledge his personal approach to, and influence on, the games we have enjoyed against the Wanderers. It was a joy to play against him — and to watch him play. We are sorry that he has now retired and that we shall not play against him again.

The second individual is remembered for a rather different reason — for runs against us. His name is Keith Crabtree and his scores against us for the Bristol University Academicals between 1965 and 1974 were: 55, 109*, 64*, 65*, 93, 30, 85, 55, 12 and 49 — an average of 88! It was no wonder that we remember him — and remember him in 1968 (with not a little pleasure) throwing his cap on the ground in despair and jumping on it as Ansell and Dalton moved relentlessly on to their opening stand of 167.

A good team could be selected from our opponents over the years. Excluding students, it might come from the following twelve:

> Crabtree (Bristol University Academicals)
> Austin (Southampton University Academic Staff)
> Russell (Shiplake Wanderers)
> Messenger (Reading Lawyers)
> Ledlie (RAF Shinfield)
> Eggar (Shiplake Wanderers) Captain
> Dindar (Reading School All Stars)
> Davis (Reading School All Stars)
> Owen (Reading School All Stars)
> Crawford (Wokingham)
> Hicks (Leckford)
> Ashton (Bristol University Academicals)

It would be a powerful side by any standards and would *have* to be captained by John Eggar. Others in the Club will no doubt wish to dispute this team and may even want to pick our own best XI to 'meet' our opponents. I leave it to them!

In addition to opponents, there are many others to whom any cricket club must be grateful and without whom no cricket would be possible. First and foremost there are groundsmen who prepare our wickets and look after pavilions. At the University we have had a succession of good groundsmen who have also been our friends: 'Sandy' Saunders, Frank Stokes,

Barry Webb and John Smith. Most of the large scores that have been made by and against us have been on our own wickets, which is testimony in itself to these groundsmen and to those who have helped them — not least Ron Mullins and the recently retired Jack Organ — to whom we presented an inscribed tankard in appreciation of 22 years of service. We have also, of course, had the pleasure of playing on other grounds, some of them with superb wickets, like Reading School and Christ Church, Oxford; others, charming cricket grounds in their own right like Shiplake College, and the cherry-lined Leckford in Hampshire. Many others could be mentioned. We have enjoyed ourselves on most of them.

We are grateful also to all those who have 'scored' for us: in the early days George Bisset and Fred England (in the Single Wicket Tournaments); John Giles through the seventies; in 1979 the painstaking Adrian Pell — and over the years, of course many players, and none more often than Bob Pearce.

With the notable exception of Bob Cook in the mid sixties, RUASCC has never enjoyed the luxury of a regular umpire, but many players and others have 'stood' for us. We have been more fortunate with 'tea ladies' who have often had to do the job in indifferent conditions. It would be invidious (if not positively dangerous!) to mention names — although some have certainly done more than their share. We are grateful to them all and welcome the adoption in recent years of a players' tea-rota which has shared the burden more equitably.

Finally, returning to the game itself, no account of the Club's history would be complete without brief reference to the special events in which we have taken part. In the early days the Single Wicket Tournament took pride of place, the winners and runners-up are recorded with the account of each season and in the records section. Most of the winners were all-rounders. The first was Keith Robinson, while Australian Max Heslehurst and David Ansell both won the tournament twice, although occasionally there was a surprise. Successful as this tournament (and the social that followed it) was, it had never been easy (in the days of a limited playing strength) to organise, and eventually it gave way to the increasing number of orthodox fixtures.

In the late 1960s and early 1970s short tours became the vogue and RUASCC travelled to Bristol and Cardiff in 1968, to Southampton in 1969, to Bristol and Cirencester in 1972 and 1973 and, on a rain-spoiled trip, to Bristol and Cardiff in 1974. The Club did not often win on these tours, but had some extraordinarily good times. More recently tours, as such, have been replaced by the Sir George Edwards Trophy games which have been played since 1975. The trophy is played for by four university staff sides. Surrey University Staff won and retained the trophy for its first three years; RUASCC won it in 1978 and 1979. Reading, Surrey and Southampton have played on all eight occasions and Reading has hosted the Trophy three times.

Whether we have been involved in ordinary fixtures, tours and tournaments, however, all of these occasions have had one thing in common: they are all essentially about the pleasure of playing cricket — with the unique combination of skill and luck, good sportsmanship and tension that this very special game offers. Inevitably there are moments of disappointment for individuals and for teams, but the dominant reflection — certainly for the author — on looking back across the many matches that are recorded in this book — is one of immense enjoyment and of great friendships. Presumably, if those two things did not exist, players would be less willing to devote as much time to the game as they do. It goes on for a long time; from May to September; and on match days from early afternoon, when the dressing room banter starts, until 'stumps' at 7.30. Then it continues into the evening, until (in the words of our Abingdon friends) the ABL is consumed, and sometimes the AFL.

It is difficult, of course, to recapture fully all of this spirit of enjoyment in the written word, sometimes long after the event — but, hopefully, the 'Gallery of Sporting Prints' at the end of this book will help the reader to do so. For RUASCC it has all been going for quite a long time now; to be as imprecise as academics often are, for 'about twenty-five years'.

1964

Captain: A Harrison
Vice Captain: A. K. Giles
Team Secretary: B. Loughborough

Played 14 Won 7 Lost 5 Drawn 2

This was a significant season in the Club's development. Alan Harrison followed Syd Fox as captain, bringing with him the experience gained with Caversham C. C. It is doubtful if we have ever had a shrewder captain. For the first time, this season, the Club kept a score book, had a printed fixture card, bought a complete set of gear and frequently provided umpires. Only 5 out of 14 games were lost. The Students' 2nd XI was beaten twice — a young man named Ansell getting a 'duck' against us in one of these games — and in the return games it was pleasing to reverse heavy defeats by Reading Police and Ian Fletcher's Particulars. Getting away with a draw at Wokingham was to prove, over subsequent years, to have been a rare event. Wally Redfern, John Lucas and Keith Robinson were the principal bowlers, and the author scored more runs — and bowled fewer overs — than he has done in later seasons.

Batting 1964

	Matches	Innings	N. O.	Runs	H. Score	Av.
A. K. Giles	10	10	2	295	51	36.8
G. A. Urquhart	7	4	2	52	25*	26.0
S. D. Smith	9	8	0	168	68	20.2
J. R. Lucas	6	6	2	68	20*	17.0
W. D. Redfern	14	13	1	198	34	16.5
D. R. Thomas	7	7	1	92	32*	15.3
A. Harrison	12	10	0	149	46	14.9
B. L. Evans	6	5	1	40	26*	10.0
F. Robertson	8	5	1	27	11	6.7
M. A. Utton	6	6	2	22	11	5.5
C. R. Pidgeon	6	5	0	22	13	4.4
B. Loughborough	11	8	1	30	9	4.3

Also batted: R. Tiwari 46; I. Fletcher 4; F. H. Anderson 20, 43*;
F. G. Stokes 9, 0; J. E. Thomas 24; K. R. Gladdish 8*, 1*, 1, 5;
J. Butler 10, 2, 0, 1; M. J. Baines 0, 4*, 0; I. P. Williams 3, 1, 0*, 0;
K. Robinson o*, 0; J. Norris 47*; Robins 0; Wright 1; Stevenson 15, 0;
De Grouchy 6*; Price 1.

Bowling 1964

	Overs	Mdns	Runs	Wkts	Av.	Best
J. R. Lucas	70.2	17	162	17	9.5	5-29
K. Robinson	62.5	13	160	14	11.4	4-25
I. P. Williams	37.3	5	156	10	15.6	2-15
A. Harrison	31	4	97	6	16.2	2-23
W. D. Redfern	102	8	318	18	17.7	3-18
B. Loughbrough	27	3	98	5	19.7	2-15
D. R. Thomas	20	1	88	2	44.0	2-13

Also bowled: A. K. Giles 8-3-25-1; J. E. Thomas 9-1-44-4;
J. Norris 19-5-42-5; J. Butler 5-1-18-1; Wright 18-5-41-2;
F. G. Stokes 14-1-52-4; Godfreys 9-0-43-0.
Regular Wicket Keeper: F. Robertson

Matches 1964

Date		Opponent	Score	Result
2 May	H	Students' 2nd XI 124-4 dec.	RUASCC 128-8 Giles 41, Harrison 27	Won by 2 wickets
6 May	A	RUASCC 57	Reading Police 58-1	Lost by 9 wickets
13 May	A	Newbury 51 Robinson 4-17 Lucas 4-6	RUASCC 52-1 Redfern 23* Lucas 20*	Won by 9 wickets
20 May	A	East Tytherley 116 Norris 5-42	RUASCC 101 Norris 47	Lost by 15 runs
27 May	A	Wokingham 151-8 dec.	RUASCC 92-8 Redfern 34	Drawn
4 June	H	Employees 71-8 Robinson 3-33 Redfern 3-18	RUASCC 74-1 Giles 40* Thomas 32*	Won (limited overs)
10 June	H	RUASCC 137 Smith 44 Evans 26*	Students' 2nd XI 82 Redfern 3-20 Robinson 4-25	Won by 55 runs
16 June	A	RUASCC 93-5 dec. Redfern 31 Urquhart 25*	S. M. S. Hermitage 94-2	Lost by 8 wickets
24 June	H	RUASCC 150 Smith 68 Redfern 33	Newbury 126-9 Robinson 3-35 Lucas 3-49	Drawn
27 June	H	RUASCC 111 Harrison 25 Thomas R. 25	Particulars 112-1	Lost by 9 wickets
1 July	H	RUASCC 188-7 dec. Harrison 46 Giles 46, Tiwari 46*	Particulars 114 Thomas J. 4-22	Won by 74 runs
7 July	A	RUASCC 119 Giles 30	Southampton University Academic Staff 121-3	Lost by 7 wickets
9 July	H	Employees 85-3	RUASCC 89-4 Giles 48*	Won (limited overs)

15 July	H	Reading Police 109	RUASCC 110-3	Won by
		Lucas 5-29	Giles 51	7 wickets
		Stokes 3-25	Anderson 40*	

1965

Captain: A. K. Giles
Vice Captain: W. D. Redfern
Team Secretary: D. R. Thomas
Fixture Secretary: B. Loughborough

Played 22 Won 7 Lost 8 Drawn 7

Final of the first Single Wicket Tournament
K. Robinson beat A. Harrison

With a policy, at this stage of the Club's history, of electing a different captain each season, Tony Giles took over the captaincy from Alan Harrison. The secretary's job was subdivided, with Roy Thomas acting as team secretary and Brian Loughborough continuing to arrange the fixtures. These increased considerably and for the first time the Club played throughout July as well as in May and June. New opponents included several Service sides, and the Students' 1st XI were beaten for the only time in the history of this fixture. Long spells of tight bowling by Flower and Robinson confined the students to 143 for 7 which the staff overtook for the loss of 6 wickets thanks to an undefeated 72 by Bob Barnwell in one of his rare appearances for RUASCC.

Although 15 of its 22 games were won or drawn a number of opponents proved to be too strong for the Club at this stage of its development. Several heavy defeats were inflicted — notably by Southampton University Academic Staff, whose 226 for 4 remains amongst the highest totals registered against the Club, and by R. A. F. Benson. The batting had to rely too often on Giles, Harrison and Wally Redfern and the bowling on Keith Robinson and Redfern. Alan Harrison topped the bowling averages, his 7 for 24 bringing a close victory at Newbury. In the return match Newbury's David Lloyd, with 83 runs and 5 wickets for 9 runs virtually won the game by himself. A sight that will always be remembered by those who saw it was Alan Harrison's punishing innings of 82 against Bristol Academicals. Elmhurst Road wasn't safe to be in!

Although never a regular player for RUASCC the Berkshire County fast bowler, John Flower, had his first games for the Club this season. Frequently the fielding was unable to give him the support he needed. One new player, however, who in due course was to play an important role in the Club's life was Bob Willey. His 7 for 11 against the Employees was a foretaste of things to come.

K. Robinson — always a good batsman as well as a superb bowler — was the hot favourite to win the Club's first single wicket tournament. He duly beat Alan Harrison in the final to receive the winner's trophy at a Social and Dance held in the Pavilion.

It is a remarkable fact that (at the time of writing) the existing ninth and tenth wicket record scores were set up in this season.

Batting 1965

	Matches	Innings	N. O.	Runs	H. Score	Av.
A. K. Giles	21	21	5	530	85	33.1
A. Harrison	13	13	0	348	82	26.8
D. R. Thomas	15	15	5	184	47*	18.4
J. E. Thomas	6	3	1	33	19	16.5
W. D. Redfern	21	20	3	263	44	15.5
K. Robinson	9	9	1	117	41	14.6
R. W. Willey	9	7	3	58	49	14.5
S. D. Smith	10	10	0	128	28	12.8
J. E. Flower	5	5	0	51	29	10.2
F. Robertson	13	10	2	76	26	9.5
M. A. Utton	8	8	0	66	26	8.2
B. Loughbrough	21	16	2	119	28*	8.1
M. J. Bains	7	6	1	40	17	8.0
F. G. Stokes	15	13	1	90	27	7.5
G. A. Urquhart	12	10	2	57	24	7.1
J. B. Dent	7	7	0	39	18	5.6
S. Fox	5	4	0	18	10	4.5
A. J. Pretlove	5	3	0	8	6	2.7
I. P. Williams	11	8	3	12	8	2.4

Also batted: R. Barnwell 72; F. H. Anderson 1*, 31; R. Tiwari 14, 31, 16; I. Fletcher 10, 2*; P. M. Harris 5; B. L. Evans 1, 6, 5; J. M. Hollas 0, 2*; Wright 21*.

Bowling 1965

	Overs	Mdns	Runs	Wkts	Av.	Best
A. Harrison	60	13	196	24	8.2	7-24
J. E. Flower	47.1	13	114	13	8.8	4-47
R. W. Willey	52.5	12	148	14	10.6	7-11
K. Robinson	112.5	19	317	22	14.4	4-30
F. G. Stokes	64	3	293	17	17.2	4-47
W. D. Redfern	153.5	23	505	29	17.4	5-37
B. Loughbrough	66	1	276	9	30.67	3-50
J. E. Thomas	57	7	194	6	32.33	2-17
A. J. Pretlove	18	3	54	1	54.00	1-4
I. P. Williams	42	6	182	3	60.67	2-45

Also bowled: G. A. Urquhart 33-0-14-2; A. K. Giles 2-0-9-1;
D. Smith 3-0-11-1; M. J. Baines 6-0-36-1; S. Fox 2-2-11-0;
D. R. Thomas 1-0-1-0; Wright 12-0-53-6; George 2-0-19-1;
M. A. Utton 4-0-19-1.
In the match v. Nautical College, Pangbourne, no analyses were kept, but
the following took wickets: W. D. Redfern (2); G. Urquhart (1);
B. Loughbrough (1).
Regular Wicket Keepers: F. Robertson and A. K. Giles

Matches 1965

28 April	H	RUASCC 149-4 dec. Giles 49	Students' 2nd XI 137-6	Drawn	
5 May	A	Wokingham 140-8 dec.	RUASCC 86	Lost by 54 runs	
6 May	H	R. A. F. Shinfield 78 Harrison 6-29	RUASCC 80-4	Won by 6 wickets	
12 May	A	RUASCC 113 Harrison 39	Newbury 96 Harrison 7-24	Won by 17 runs	
15 May	A	Staff College Owls 156-8 dec. Stokes 4-47	RUASCC 120 Redfern 43	Lost by 36 runs	
19 May	H	RUASCC 153-9 dec. Giles 57 Harrison 55	East Tytherley 122-8	Drawn	
26 May	H	RUASCC 87 Giles 32 Harrison 29	S. M. S. Hermitage 88-4	Lost by 6 wickets	
29 May	H	RUASCC 181-7 dec. Giles 85	Employees 178-9	Drawn	
2 June	H	RUASCC 183-6 dec.	Students' 2nd XI 75 Robinson 4-20	Won by 108 runs	
9 June	A	RUASCC 148-5 dec. Giles 58*	S. M. S. Hermitage 107-7 Robinson 4-30	Drawn	
12 June	H	RUASCC 146-6 dec.	Students' 2nd XI 100 Redfern 5-37	Won by 46 runs	
14 June	H	Nautical College Staff Pangbourne 149-9 dec.	RUASCC 125-9 Willey 49	Drawn	
19 June	A	RUASCC 100	Reading Casuals 85-4	Drawn	
23 June	H	Newbury 139-7 dec. Lloyd 83	RUASCC 90 Lloyd 5-9	Lost by 49 runs	
26 June	H	Employees 71 Willey 7-11	RUASCC 72-5	Won by 5 wickets	

29 June	H	Students' 1st XI 143-7 dec. Flower 4-47	RUASCC 144-6 Barnwell 72*	Won by 4 wickets
30 June	H	Bristol University Academicals 188-3 dec.	RUASCC 147-6 Harrison 82	Drawn
3 July	H	RUASCC 122 R. Thomas 47*	Particulars 123-6 Redfern 5-37	Lost by 4 wickets
6 July	H	Southampton University Academic Staff 226-4 dec. Burton 79, Small 72* Harrison 3-48	RUASCC 132	Lost by 94 runs
14 July	H	RUASCC 166-8 dec.	Reading Police 119 Wright 6-53	Won by 47 runs
22 July	H	RUASCC 72 Urquhart 24	A. Harrison's XI 74-8	Lost by 2 wickets
28 July	H	R. A. F. Benson 177-8 Redfern 3-37	RUASCC 43	Lost by 134 runs

1966

Captain: W. D. Redfern
Vice Captain: B. Loughbrough
Team Secretary: R. W. Willey
Fixture Secretary: A. Harrison

Played 20 Won 4 Lost 10 Drawn 6

Final of Single Wicket Tournament:
A. K. Giles beat W. D. Redfern

Wally Redfern took over the captaincy. Without the advantage
of the same amount of experience of the job as his predecessors,
his task was made especially difficult by a side which managed
to get dismissed for less than 100 in no fewer than 8 of its
20 matches. Even when it put together a good score (203 in
the final match) it was unable to dismiss the opposition. No
regular batsman could reach an average of 20. Bob Willey's
41 wickets put him well ahead of his nearest rivals and Redfern
himself frequently contributed well with bat and ball. David
Ansell played his first three games for the Club — the first of
many to come. A new fixture, which has lasted over the years,
was Leckford, near Stockbridge, from whom we suffered two
defeats and first met the redoubtable fast bowler, Hicks. His
4 for 29 and 4 for 17 were the first of many wickets he would
take against us — but we enjoyed our first bite of the cherries
that grow around this delightful Hampshire ground. Keith
Crabtree, of the Bristol University Academicals, scored his
first century against us (109) and began his own remarkable
run of high scores against us, whilst his colleague Ashton
(61 and 6 for 24) remains (like Hicks) one of the best quick

bowlers we have ever faced. With only one victory between early June and the end of July, this was not a vintage year so far as results were concerned — but there was the usual enjoyment, nevertheless. The 99 scored by Bob Willey and Keith Dugdale against Reading Police remains a Club record for the seventh wicket.

Batting 1966

	Matches	Innings	N. O.	Runs	H. Score	Av.
R. Tiwari	9	9	0	301	71	33.4
A. K. Giles	13	13	1	210	40	17.5
R. W. Willey	18	16	6	150	60	15.0
W. D. Redfern	18	16	2	193	27	13.8
A. J. Pretlove	8	8	1	94	34*	13.4
A. Harrison	15	15	0	179	45	11.9
F. G. Stokes	9	8	0	88	30	11.0
J. K. Dugdale	6	5	2	31	26*	10.3
I. P. Williams	11	8	2	55	37	9.2
J. B. Dent	6	5	0	43	20	8.6
Josef	5	5	0	38	26	7.6
G. A. Urquhart	10	10	2	60	19*	7.5
B. Loughbrough	17	16	1	90	22	6.0
M. J. Baines	7	7	1	28	12*	4.7
C. W. Chalkin	8	7	1	20	6*	3.3

Also batted: R. Barnwell 25; J. E. Flower 0, 48; D. J. Ansell 1, 44, 0;
K. Robinson 6, 3; D. R. Thomas 5, 4; K. Simkiss 7*; F. H. Anderson 0, 0*;
M. A. Utton 0; G. Willey 0, 0, 0, 1; E. J. T. Collins 1*, 0, 1*, 0; Philips 12;
Parsons 32, 0, 8, 5; House 4; Mathur 4; Jarrow 2; Sinah 1; Sillitoe 0.

Bowling 1966

	Overs	Mdns	Runs	Wkts	Av.	Best
R. W. Willey	188	35	560	41	13.7	5-7
K. Robinson	31	4	96	7	13.7	5-43
F. G. Stokes	38	4	198	14	14.1	5-38
A. Harrison	42.1	5	139	9	15.4	4-26
W. D. Redfern	150.4	26	520	32	16.2	6-27
J. E. Flower	24	5	69	4	17.2	4-24
A. J. Pretlove	23.2	3	88	5	17.6	3-17
I. P. Williams	26	1	113	6	18.8	2-32
B. Loughbrough	60.5	5	256	13	19.7	4-34

Also bowled: D. R. Thomas 10-0-41-2; E. J. T. Collins 4-0-38-1;
D. J. Ansell 3-0-26-0; G. Willey 3-0-7-0; J. K. Dugdale 2-0-10-0.
Regular Wicket Keeper: A. K. Giles

Matches 1966

27 April	H	RUASCC 75	Students' 2nd XI 79-5	Lost by 5 wickets
9 May	H	R. A. F. Shinfield 81-7 dec.	RUASCC 55	Lost by 26 runs
14 May	A	RUASCC 121	Staff College Owls 45 Redfern 5-24 Willey 4-16	Won by 76 runs
16 May	H	Employees 79 Willey 5-7	RUASCC 83-3	Won by 7 wickets
18 May	A	RUASCC 67	Wallingford 71-6	Lost by 4 wickets
28 May+	H	RUASCC 63	Leckford 64-2	Lost by 8 wickets
1 June	H	RUASCC 185 Tiwari 71	Students' 2nd XI 182-9	Drawn
6 June	A	Nautical College Staff Pangbourne 145-6 dec.	RUASCC 90-6	Drawn
8 June	A	S. M. S. Hermitage 50 Redfern 6-27	RUASCC 51-5	Won by 5 wickets
11 June	H	Students' 2nd XI 143	RUASCC 41 Glester 8-12	Lost by 102 runs
14 June	A	R. A. F. Shinfield 131	RUASCC 92	Lost by 39 runs
19 June	A	Leckford 116 Loughbrough 4-34	RUASCC 66	Lost by 50 runs
22 June	H	RUASCC 156-9 dec. Ansell 44, Giles 40	Newbury 157-4	Lost by 6 wickets
25 June	H	Employees 55-5		Abandoned as a draw
28 June	H	Students' 1st XI 165-3 dec.	RUASCC 131-9 Flower 48	Drawn
29 June	A	Bristol University Academicals 199-5 dec. Crabtree 109* Ashton 61	RUASCC 75 Ashton 6-24	Lost by 124 runs

12 July	A	RUASCC 154 Tiwari 43	Southampton University Academic Staff 130-9 Willey 5-37 Harrison 4-26	Drawn
13 July	H	RUASCC 134 Willey 60	Reading Police 135-3	Lost by 7 wickets
26 July	H	Leeds University Academic Staff 152-7 dec.	RUASCC 153-4 Tiwari 62	Won by 6 wickets
27 July	H	RUASCC 203 Tiwari 71	R. A. F. Benson 152-8 Stokes 4-24	Drawn

+ This match was followed by a limited overs match in which the scores were Leckford 65-2, RUASCC 65-4. Match tied.

1967

Captain: A. Harrison
Vice Captain: R. W. Willey
Team Secretary: I. P. Williams
Fixture Secretary: A. Harrison

Played 21 Won 6 Lost 9 Drawn 4 Tied 2

Final of Single Wicket Tournament:
B. D. Dore beat S. D. Smith

Despite the recall of Alan Harrison to skipper the side and
the arrival on the scene of numerous players who, in due
course, were to make massive contributions to the playing
strength of the Club, only one fewer game was lost than in
the previous season.

Never before — or since — have so many talented cricketers
joined the Club in one season. Graham Dalton — a giant of a
player; David Robertson — arguably, when he allowed himself
to be, one of the most accomplished batsman we have had;
Mike Sewell, in due course to become our most prolific run
getter and studious captain; John Ford and Colin Walker,
neither of them able to play too often, but both of them highly
talented performers who seemed not to need the help of nets or
match practice to succeed. In addition, David Ansell had his
first full season for the Club, and from time to time Barry Dore
unleashed his particular brand of unpredictable fast bowling,
which was effective enough on his day for him to win the
single wicket trophy.

With this influx of talent, the season started well, the side not losing until the seventh match. Giles, Harrison, and Redfern continued, in their different ways, to score runs, but were now supported by the newcomers, especially by Graham Dalton (who scored the first '50' of his life) and David Robertson. Graham Dalton and Bob Willey bore the brunt of the bowling, with Keith Robinson, John Flower, John Ford and Wally Redfern all bowling well at times.

Beating Wokingham at Wokingham was a rare event, although scoring the necessary 45 runs was never straightforward. After a bad mid season patch there were enjoyable games against three other University Staff sides resulting in victory over Leeds (Robertson and Dalton scoring 99 for the second wicket), a one wicket defeat by Southampton, and an honourable draw against Bristol — Crabtree 64 not out. In the final game against R. A. F. Shinfield a Wing Commander Ledlie gave us an education in scoring 104 not out. A disappointing season, perhaps, but a side with talents which before long would achieve more.

Batting 1967

	Matches	Innings	N. O.	Runs	H. Score	Av.
G. E. Dalton	16	14	1	396	53	30.5
A. K. Giles	16	16	3	323	58*	24.9
D. H. Robertson	16	16	1	331	69	22.1
M. J. Sewell	10	10	2	155	39	19.4
F. Robertson	7	2	1	15	11*	15.0
A. Harrison	18	16	2	192	65	13.7
F. G. Stokes	8	8	2	80	43*	13.3
W. D. Redfern	17	15	4	140	23	12.7
R. W. Wiley	17	14	2	129	38	10.7
C. H. Walker	5	5	2	31	12	10.3
D. J. Ansell	18	16	1	137	41*	9.1
J. K. Dugdale	6	6	4	17	8*	8.5
K. Robinson	5	5	1	32	15	8.0
G. A. Urquhart	7	5	0	38	13	7.6
D. Smith	6	6	1	36	13*	7.2
I. P. Williams	12	7	1	23	12	3.8
B. D. Dore	10	4	1	5	3	1.7
R. Mead	8	4	0	6	3	1.5

Also batted: J. E. Flower 27, 2; A. J. Pretlove 0, 11, 5*; G. Kirkby 6; M. Dawson 6; J. A. Ford 3, 12, 0; P. M. Harris 5.

Bowling 1967

	Overs	Mdns	Runs	Wkts	Av.	Best
J. A. Ford	19	2	52	8	6.5	5-25
J. E. Flower	38	10	95	12	7.9	8-29
D. H. Robertson	24	3	126	10	12.6	3-13
F. G. Stokes	24.3	2	97	7	13.9	2-8
R. W. Willey	124	26	426	26	16.4	4-7
K. Robinson	58	12	166	10	16.6	4-42
G. E. Dalton	139	25	424	25	16.9	5-22
B. D. Dore	28	2	105	5	21.0	2-34
D. J. Ansell	51	4	208	9	23.1	3-36
W. D. Redfern	65.3	9	233	10	23.3	3-7

Also bowled: A. K. Giles 3-0-8-1; G. Kirby 4-0-24-2; I. P. Williams 5-0-28-2; A. J. Pretlove 7-0-38-1; A. Harrison 6-0-22-0.

Regular Wicket Keepers: F. Robertson and A. K. Giles

Matches 1967

3 May	A	Wokingham 45 D. Robertson 3-13	RUASCC 49-5 Willey 21	Won by 5 wickets
6 May	H	RUASCC 137-7 dec. Willey 38 Dalton 37 Giles 25	ICI Bozedown House 88 Dalton 4-17 Willey 4-25	Won by 49 runs
10 May	H	RUASCC 161 Harrison 65 Dalton 32 Giles 26	Particulars 96-9 Willey 4-7 Dalton 3-29	Drawn
15 May	H	RUASCC 87-3 (20 overs) Ansell 41*	Employees 65-5 (20 overs) Ford 3-27	Won by 22 runs
22 May	H	ICI Bozedown House 81-6 Ford 5-25	RUASCC 81-8 Giles 38*	Tied (18 overs)
31 May	H	RUASCC 158-8 dec. Dalton 48 Stokes 43*	S. M. S. Hermitage 78	Won by 80 runs
3 June	H	RUASCC 102 Sewell 27	Students' 2nd XI 105-3	Lost by 7 wickets
6 June	A	RUASCC 104-4 Dalton 44	Nautical College Staff Pangbourne 104-5	Tied (20 overs)
12 June	H	RUASCC 111-3 D. Robertson 46* Giles 36*	Employees 114-7 Ansell 3-36 Willey 4-48	Lost by 3 wickets (limited overs)
14 June	A	East Tytherley 141-5 dec.	RUASCC 105 D. Robertson 40	Lost by 36 runs
18 June	A	Leckford 173-6 dec. D. Robertson 3-31	RUASCC 105-6 Giles 58*	Drawn
21 June	A	RUASCC 202-8 dec. Dalton 52 Giles 37 D. Robertson 34	Newbury 136-5	Drawn

27 June	H	RUASCC 63	Students' 2nd XI 67-4	Lost by 6 wickets
28 June	A	S. M. S. Hermitage 86 Flower 8-29	RUASCC 76 Flower 27	Lost by 10 runs
1 July	H	RUASCC 165-7 dec. Dalton 53 Giles 36	Leckford 73 Redfern 3-7 Dalton 5-22	Won by 92 runs
4 July	H	RUASCC 75 Sewell 16 Stokes 16	Students' 1st XI 76-4	Lost by 6 wickets
5 July	H	Newbury 153-4 dec.	RUASCC not recorded Sewell 39	Lost
12 July	H	RUASCC 112 D. Robertson 32	Southampton University Academic Staff 114-9 Robinson 4-42	Lost by 1 wicket
13 July	H	RUASCC 150-9 dec. Dalton 51 D. Robertson 32	Bristol University Academicals 105-5 Dalton 4-32 Crabtree 64*	Drawn
17 July	H	Leeds University Academicals 144 Willey 4-13 Robinson 3-38	RUASCC 148-3 D. Robertson 69 Dalton 37	Won by 7 wickets
19 July	A	R. A. F. Shinfield 192-4 dec. Ledlie 104*	RUASCC 96 Willey 38	Lost by 94 runs

1968

Captain: R. W. Willey
Vice Captain: D. H. Robertson
Team Secretary: I. P. Williams
Fixture Secretary: A. Harrison

Played 17 Won 7 Lost 8 Drawn 2

Final of Single Wicket Tournament:
D. J. Ansell beat A. Harrison

Bob Willey enjoyed the first of his two years as captain. He was the first player to captain the side who had not been involved from the days when the Club first had a regular fixture list. Before his back began to give him trouble, a season or two later, he was a splendid opening bowler, a superb slip fielder and, when the mood took him, a more than capable batsman. His modest manner belied the firmness of his captaincy; he was, probably, the most under-rated captain the Club has had.

After an early defeat from Wallingford, the side enjoyed three victories, including one against Shiplake College Wanderers — a fixture that, over the years has become the one enjoyed above all others. Much of that enjoyment has emanated from the joyful approach to the game of the Shiplake Headmaster, ex-Derbyshire captain J. D. Eggar. His dismissal on this occasion for 1 was to be a rare occurrence. As the season advanced it became — not untypically — a 'fifty fifty' one. There were some good performances — including a 7 wicket win at Newbury — thanks to a stand of 118 between Dalton and Robertson for the second wicket and some bad ones including dismissal for 34 by S. M. S. Hermitage and 40 by R. A. F. Benson. The side worked hard against the Students' 1st XI, but their 198 for 9 was a bit out of reach.

A highlight of the season was Dalton's and Ansell's opening stand of 167 against the Bristol Staff (not improved upon until 1979) but the inevitable Crabtree, with 65 not out, held us off.

During the season David Robertson, Graham Dalton and David Ansell, not to mention Bob Willey, began to show more of the promise that had been hinted at in the season before. Mike Sewell, at this stage gave no real hint of the prolific batsman he was to become.

Ray Macdonald began his shortlived but highly successful playing career with the Club as an opening bowler, and the unorthodox but, at times, equally successful batting of Bob Pearce was first seen. Barry Dore, playing and bowling more than he had in the previous season produced his own particular volatile approach to using the new ball — and, at times, when he was properly harnessed, was more likely to unsettle good batsmen than most bowlers we have had. With Fred Robertson getting better and better behind the stumps as he got older, Tony Giles began his career as a variously described slow bowler.

Despite the talent that was available and growing, the variable results of this season reflected the frequent unavailability of key players. This is evidenced by the numbers who 'also batted and bowled'. Contrary to some opinions of colleagues, work did (and does) sometimes take precedence over cricket! However, the season was enjoyed — not least the two away games on consecutive days against Bristol and Cardiff University Staff teams. This was the Club's first experience of 'touring' and, of course, had its moments.

Batting 1968

	Matches	Innings	N. O.	Runs	H. Score	Av.
G. E. Dalton	14	13	1	295	67*	24.6
D. J. Ansell	13	12	0	230	70	19.2
A. Harrison	14	14	3	206	54*	18.7
D. H. Robertson	16	16	2	249	63	17.8
A. K. Giles	13	13	0	133	37	10.2
W. D. Redfern	9	7	0	47	18	6.7
M. J. Sewell	11	11	1	63	30	6.3
I. P. Williams	11	6	1	24	10	4.8
M. Mitchell	11	8	1	33	17	4.7
F. Robertson	12	11	5	27	4*	4.5
R. W. Willey	15	11	2	40	12	4.4
B. D. Dore	13	8	3	9	5	1.8

Also batted: C. H. Walker 17*, 11, 28*; P. Payne 22*, 18; S. Goonesena 29;
R. D. Pearce 13, 32; P. A. Allum 18; J. E. Flower 18; K. Robinson 14, 30, 9;
F. G. Stokes 8, 27; F. J. B. Stilwell 7; J. A. Ford 2, 7, 2;
R. Macdonald 0, 5*, 0, 1; A. Cremin 2, 4; J. Burton 0; D. H. Farmer 0;
Jackson 0.

Bowling 1968

	Overs	Mdns	Runs	Wkts	Av.	Best
R. W. Willey	120	20	336	31	10.8	5-17
B. D. Dore	49	10	141	12	11.7	3-12
R. Macdonald	54	8	160	11	14.5	5-20
D. J. Ansell	45	1	191	13	14.7	4-17
K. Robinson	38	7	120	7	17.1	3-28
G. E. Dalton	105	23	336	18	18.7	4-21
M. Mitchell	19	5	64	3	21.3	1-6
A. K. Giles	48	2	218	10	21.8	4-53

Also bowled: J. A. Ford 4-2-3-1; F. G. Stokes 12-1-40-4;
A. Cremin 14-2-48-4; I. P. Williams 5-0-14-1; S. Gonnesena 5-0-25-1;
J. E. Flower 13-1-66-2; D. H. Robertson 4-0-30-0; A. Harrison 10-1-38-0;
W. D. Redfern 12-0-66-0; Jackson 5-0-23-0.
Regular Wicket Keepers: F. Robertson and A. K. Giles

Matches 1968

15 May	A	Wallingford 166 Ansell 4-52 Willey 4-29	RUASCC 90 Goonesena 29	Lost by 76 runs
23 May	A	Shiplake College Wanderers 119-7 dec. Dalton 4-21	RUASCC 121-3 D. Robertson 57* Giles 29	Won by 7 wickets
27 May	H	Postgraduates 77-4	RUASCC 78-4 Stokes 27	Won by 6 wickets (15 overs)
29 May	A	S. M. S. Hermitage 147-9 dec. Giles 4-53 Willey 3-37	RUASCC 150-5 Harrison 54* Ansell 26, Giles 23 Payne 22*	Won by 5 wickets
1 June	H	Students' 2nd XI 151-7 dec.	RUASCC 84 Harrison 21 Ansell 20	Lost by 67 runs
10 June	H	RUASCC 81-8 Dalton 40	Employees 70-10 (12 a side) Macdonald 5-20 Willey 3-8	Won by 11 runs (15 overs)
16 June	A	RUASCC 117-9 dec. D. Robertson 63	Leckford 121-6 Willey 3-44 Macdonald 3-60	Lost by 4 wickets
19 June	A	RUASCC 106 K. Robinson 30	Newbury 108-6 Robinson 3-32	Lost by 4 wickets
26 June	A	RUASCC 34 D. Robertson 13	Hermitage 36-1	Lost by 9 wickets
29 June	H	Leckford 125-9 dec. Ansell 4-17 Dalton 4-32	RUASCC 110-9 Giles 37 Dalton 30	Drawn
30 June	A	RUASCC 110 Harrison 43, Allum 18 Giles 17	Staff College Owls 82 Dore 3-12	Won by 28 runs

2 July	H	Students' 1st XI 198-7 dec.	RUASCC 133 Ansell 38, Sewell 30	Lost by 65 runs
3 July	H	Newbury 150-8 dec.	RUASCC 154-3 Dalton 67* D. Robertson 41	Won by 7 wickets
15 July	A	RUASCC 188-5 dec. Dalton 92 Ansell 70	Bristol University Academicals 154-4 Crabtree 65*	Drawn
16 July	A	Cardiff University Staff 101 Willey 5-17, Dore 3-12	RUASCC 48 Forster 5-4	Lost by 53 runs
24 July	A	R. A. F. Benson 147-8 dec. Dore 3-20 Jackson 3-28	RUASCC 40 Pearce 13 Williams 10	Lost by 107 runs
28 July	A	RUASCC 133-8 dec. Pearce 32 Walker 28*	Hurstbourne Priors 52 Cremin 3-8 Dalton 3-11	Won by 81 runs

53

1969

Captain: R. W. Willey
Vice Captain: M. J. Sewell
Team Secretary: I. P. Williams
Fixture Secretary: A. Harrison

Played 25 Won 3 Lost 9 Drawn 13

Final of Single Wicket Tournament:
R. D. Pearce beat D. J. Ansell

A season characterised by an unusually large number of drawn games, including two on a three-match tour in the Southampton area in July and two, later in the month, when, on consecutive days, the side surpassed 200. The 243 for 4 scored at home against Abingdon has not often been exceeded.

The bowling was aided by the more regular appearances of Ray Macdonald and the resurrection, after two seasons of relative obscurity as a bowler, of Alan Harrison. But even his 5 for 7 at Hermitage could not prevent a draw. Roger Loader was the only new player to become a regular member of the Club and immediately began to make a contribution with the bat. The mainstay of the batting, however, was David Robertson who scored nearly twice as many runs as his nearest rival, including several dominating innings. Only he and Giles averaged more than 20. Bob Willey, in his second year as captain, again topped the bowling averages, well ahead of his nearest rival.

New fixtures included Reading School All Stars which has remained a friendly and popular fixture ever since. After narrowly losing the first of two games with them, a rare victory was achieved on the splendid Erleigh Road Ground, despite a score of 77 from Tony Davis.

Despite a disappointingly low number of victories, the side was well captained by Bob Willey, and Mike Sewell, as Vice Captain, had his first opportunity to handle the side. Iwan Williams concluded three years as a very efficient team secretary, and was only to play a few more games for the Club. Never one of the star performers, he was an excellent club man as player and administrator and his tenth wicket stand of 51 with fellow Welshman D. R. Thomas, scored against the Particulars in 1965, remains a Club record. They first confused and then frustrated the opposition by 'calling' in Welsh!

It was a remarkable performance for Bob Pearce who had never bowled in a match to beat David Ansell in the final of the Single Wicket Tournament.

Batting 1969

	Matches	Innings	N. O.	Runs	H. Score	Av.
D. H. Robertson	23	23	2	665	82	31.7
A. K. Giles	17	17	3	377	75	26.9
D. J. Ansell	18	18	0	332	74	18.4
R. J. Loader	15	12	3	148	29*	16.4
S. D. Smith	6	5	1	64	30*	16.0
G. E. Dalton	16	15	3	167	43	13.9
A. Harrison	18	17	0	236	84	13.9
W. D. Redfern	19	16	4	156	59*	13.0
M. J. Sewell	16	16	3	184	24	12.3
R. Macdonald	16	7	2	57	24	11.4
B. D. Dore	17	9	4	56	13*	11.2
R. D. Pearce	20	16	1	168	35	10.9
R. W. Willey	11	7	1	27	9*	4.5
F. Robertson	9	6	1	11	10*	2.2

Also batted: Kotecha 54*, 25, 42; T. Barrett 28; D. Lloyd 21; J. Challis 19;
C. H. Walker 11*, 1, 13, 9*; J. A. Ford 3, 18, 30, 6; B. McAndrew 14, 16, 6;
S. Fox 8; K. Robinson 1, 4, 3; A. R. Jones 0*, 2, 1, 1; J. E. Thomas 0;
I. P. Williams 0; Keen 22*; Murphy 0.

Bowling 1969

	Overs	Mdns	Runs	Wkts	Av.	Best
R. W. Willey	130.4	34	286	24	11.9	4-19
A. Harrison	95	13	341	18	18.9	5-7
R. Macdonald	174.2	27	665	33	20.2	5-25
G. E. Dalton	146	24	507	22	23.0	3-15
K. Robinson	68	4	277	11	25.2	4-71
B. D. Dore	70	7	285	11	25.9	3-74
W. D. Redfern	21	1	83	3	27.7	2-23
D. J. Ansell	67	4	297	7	42.4	2-25
J. A. Ford	31	7	93	2	46.5	1-15

Also bowled: Cremin 2-0-9-1; Keen 8-2-42-4; Kotecha 9-1-37-3;
T. Barrett 11-1-57-4; D. Lloyd 9-1-31-2; Murphy 5-1-31-1; J. E.
J. E. Thomas 10-3-31-1; D. H. Robertson 12-0-77-2; J. Challis 11-3-42-1;
A. R. Jones 15-2-63-1; D. Foot 3-0-25-0; A. K. Giles 13-0-51-0;
B. McAndrew 3-0-21-0; M. J. Sewell 6-0-42-0; C. H. Walker 1-0-6-0;
I. P. Williams 2-0-16-0.
Regular Wicket Keepers: A. K. Giles and F. Robertson

Matches 1969

30 April	A	Wokingham 155 Harrison 4-38	RUASCC 103-6 Smith 30	Drawn
11 May	A	Students' 2nd XI 135-7 dec.	RUASCC 125 D. Robertson 54	Lost by 10 runs
15 May	A	RUASCC 128-8 dec. D. Robertson 82	Reading School All Stars 132-7 Dalton 3-24	Lost by 3 wickets
20 May	A	RUASCC 130-6 dec. D. Robertson 40 Giles 27	Shiplake College Wanderers 123-4	Drawn
24 May	H	Employees 130-8 dec. Willey 4-26	RUASCC 36-2	Abandoned as draw
28 May	A	RUASCC 153-4 dec. D. Robertson 71 Redfern 45	S. M. S. Hermitage 86-8 Harrison 5-7	Drawn
1 June	A	Bradfield College 161-6 dec. Macdonald 4-34	RUASCC 70-4 D. Robertson 23	Drawn
4 June	A	RUASCC 87	Wallingford 46 Harrison 3-8 Willey 4-19	Won by 41 runs
11 June	A	RUASCC 176-4 dec. Kotecha 54 Giles 50	Reading School All Stars 142 Davis 77, Keen 4-42	Won by 34 runs
15 June	A	RUASCC 79	Leckford 82-4 Macdonald 4-19	Lost by 6 wickets
18 June	A	Newbury 148-6 dec. Macdonald 3-57	RUASCC 104-8 Giles 32	Drawn
25 June	A	RUASCC 106-9 dec. Kotecha 25 Sewell 24	S. M. S. Hermitage 107-7 Dalton 3-35	Lost by 3 wickets
26 June	A	RUASCC 140 Kotecha 42 Pearce 35	Abingdon 144-1	Lost by 9 wickets

Date		Home team	Away team	Result
28 June	H	RUASCC 150 D. Robertson 54 Ford 30, Loader 29	Leckford 95-8 Dalton 3-15 Willey 3-25	Drawn
29 June	A	RUASCC 180-7 dec. Giles 75 Ansell 34	Staff College Owls 140 Macdonald 5-25 Harrison 3-34	Won by 40 runs
1 July	A	Students' 1st XI 169 Seager 100	RUASCC 56	Lost by 113 runs
2 July	H	Newbury 236-4 dec. Lloyd 106* Macdonald 3-74	RUASCC 125 Pearce 34 Giles 28	Lost by 111 runs
8 July	A	RUASCC 175-5 dec. D. Robertson 73 Ansell 56	Southampton College of Technology 130-5 Dore 3-34	Drawn
9 July	A	Flamingo C. C. 176-6 Dalton 3-40	RUASCC 133-8 D. Robertson 34 Pearce 30	Drawn
10 July	A	RUASCC 113-9 dec.	Southampton University Academic Staff 115-1	Lost by 9 wickets
12 July	H	Cardiff University Staff 224-4 dec.	RUASCC 175-4 Ansell 74	Drawn
14 July	H	Bristol University Academicals 173-8 dec. Crabtree 93 Robinson 4-71	RUASCC 114-6 Giles 56	Drawn
23 July	H	RUASCC 214-8 dec. D. Robertson 58 Barrett 28 Harrison 25	RAF Benson 170-8	Drawn
24 July	H	RUASCC 243-4 dec. Harrison 84 Ansell 46, Dalton 43	Abingdon 190-8 Robinson 3-57	Drawn
27 July	A	Hurstbourne Priors 206-4 dec. North 91, Redfern 3-23	RUASCC 105 Redfern 59	Lost by 101 runs

1970

Captain: A. K. Giles
Vice Captain and Team Secretary: D. J. Ansell
Fixture Secretary: A. Harrison
Assistant Fixture Secretary: D. H. Robertson
Treasurer: R. J. Loader
Social Member: B. D. Dore

Played 20 Won 5 Lost 6 Drawn 9

Final of Single Wicket Tournament:
M. R. Heslehurst beat R. D. Pearce

Captained for a second term of office by Tony Giles, the
playing record was a slight improvement on the previous
year — but the Club still did not find winning easy. This was
largely because three bowlers who, in the previous season,
had bowled 450 overs between them — and each of them about
twice as many overs as any other player — were no longer
available. Bob Willey went on secondment to Australia,
Graham Dalton to Nigeria and Ray Macdonald left Reading
for good. That the record was as good as it was, owed much,
so far as the attack was concerned, to the more regular
appearances of Keith Robinson, the more steady form of
Barry Dore and the increased use of David Ansell as a stock
bowler.

With the bat, David Robertson continued to lead the way —
often when others failed — and his 98 not out against the
Employees was the nearest, to date, that anyone in the Club
had come to scoring a century. David Ansell's earlier promise

with the bat was now being fulfilled and the redoutable
Jim Knowlson — some years previously of Students' 1st XI
fame — not only took over behind the stumps, but averaged
over 20 runs an innings. Many opponents were to discover
over the years (and still are discovering) how difficult he is to
dislodge. Max Heslehurst came to us from Queensland, in
place of Bob Willey, and gradually found his form as an all
rounder — in time to win the Single Wicket Tournament from
Bob Pearce. Another valuable newcomer was Dave Foot —
never a 'prolific' cricketer but a wonderful Club member —
and a quite fearless fielder.

The only new fixture was Woodley. Thanks to 17 accurate
overs from Keith Robinson (for 42) the Students' 1st XI was
contained to 142 for 8 and when rain stopped the match with
the staff score at 17 for 0, things looked promising. The
Shiplake match looked lost after the Club crawled to 138 in
rather a long time and Shiplake had 97 on the board before
the fourth wicket fell. A spell of 6 for 18 by Giles then
turned the match around, with Shiplake holding off defeat
at 132 for 9. Another destructive spell of bowling which
failed to produce victory was Keith Robinson's 8 for 48
against Newbury. In a drawn match against our Bristol
counterparts, Crabtree was confined to a mere 30.

The administration of the Club was strengthened in this
season by the appointment, for the first time, of an Assistant
Fixture Secretary, a Treasurer and a Social Member. At the
same time, with eleven members playing in more than half
the fixtures, the side began (despite the loss of several key
players) perhaps to look and play more like a team, than
hitherto in its history.

Batting 1970

	Matches	Innings	N. O.	Runs	H. Score	Av.
J. A. Ford	7	6	3	105	32	35.0
D. H. Robertson	15	14	1	435	98*	33.5
D. J. Ansell	16	16	1	413	85	27.5
J. R. Knowlson	14	11	0	227	60	20.6
K. Robinson	10	6	4	41	12*	20.5
A. Harrison	8	7	1	98	51	16.3
A. K. Giles	16	15	4	171	65	15.5
C. H. Walker	6	6	2	60	29	15.0
M. J. Sewell	17	16	1	222	30	14.8
W. D. Redfern	16	14	2	157	31	13.1
R. J. Loader	12	12	1	132	41	12.0
M. R. Heslehurst	16	15	3	132	28*	11.0
R. D. Pearce	16	16	3	138	29	10.6
A. R. Jones	8	5	2	9	2*	3.0
B. D. Dore	15	8	4	3	2*	0.7

Also batted: D. Smith 28; I. P. Williams 16, 2; Gibson 7; F. Robertson 7, 6; Griffin 6; D. H. S. Foot 4, 9, 2*, 2; J. E. Thomas 5; J. K. Dugdale 5; Jackson 5; S. Fox 2; R. D. Stern 1*; A. J. Pretlove 0.

Bowling 1970

	Overs	Mdns	Runs	Wkts	Av.	Best
A. K. Giles	34	3	154	15	10.3	6-18
K. Robinson	162	41	439	39	11.3	8-48
J. A. Ford	59	8	199	9	22.1	3-50
A. R. Jones	46	3	218	9	24.2	3-56
A. Harrison	21	3	74	3	24.7	1-14
B. D. Dore	145	28	600	24	25.0	4-6
W. D. Redfern	45	8	160	6	26.7	2-28
D. H. Robertson	32	1	86	3	28.7	1-11
D. J. Ansell	73	7	321	11	29.2	3-64
M. R. Heslehurst	40	2	196	6	32.7	4-41

Also bowled: J. E. Thomas 15-3-33-8; Jackson 4-1-14-1; Griffin 9-1-37-2; J. R. Knowlson 2-0-15-0; C. H. Walker 1-0-3-0; R. D. Pearce 1-0-14-0. Regular Wicket Keeper: J. R. Knowlson

Matches 1970

29 April	A	RUASCC 101-9 dec. D. Robertson 40	Wokingham 102-3	Lost by 7 wickets
14 May	A	RUASCC 190-7 dec. Harrison 51 D. Robertson 38 Ford 32*, Giles 26	Reading School All Stars 106-6 Thomas 3-13	Drawn
16 May	H	Students' 2nd XI 120 K. Robinson 6-19 Dore 3-23	RUASCC 121-5 D. Robertson 31 Heslehurst 28*	Won by 5 wickets
19 May	A	RUASCC 138 Ansell 56	Shiplake College Wanderers 132-9 Giles 6-18	Drawn Drawn
25 May	H	RUASCC 214-6 dec. D. Robertson 98* Harrison 32 Redfern 31	Employees 129 Thomas 5-22 Dore 4-7	Won by 85 runs
27 May	A	RUASCC 82 D. Robertson 24 Ansell 16	S. M. S. Hermitage 82-3	Lost by 7 wickets
3 June	A	RUASCC 190-8 Knowlson 60 Loader 40 D. Robertson 27	Wallingford 150-6	Drawn
10 June	A	Reading School All Stars 200-7 dec.	RUASCC 116-9 D. Robertson 41	Drawn
14 June	A	RUASCC 192-8 dec. Giles 65 D. Robertson 27 Redfern 25*	Leckford 193-3 Jones 3-56	Lost by 7 wickets
17 June	A	Newbury 144 Robinson 8-48	RUASCC 99-9 Sewell 31 D. Robertson 19	Drawn
24 June	A	RUASCC 105-4 dec. Ansell 60	S. M. S. Hermitage 106-3	Lost by 7 wickets

25 June	A	RUASCC 103 Knowlson 23 Heslehurst 21	Abingdon 106-2		Lost by 8 wickets
27 June	H	Leckford 160-7 dec. Harding 100 Ansell 3-64, Ford 3-50	RUASCC 162-4 Ansell 85 Sewell 30		Won by 6 wickets
28 June	A	Staff College Owls 143	RUASCC 142-9 Ansell 39 D. Robertson 28		Drawn
30 June	H	Students' 1st XI 142-8 dec. Dore 4-34	RUASCC 17-0		Match abandoned as a draw
1 July	H	Newbury 182-8 dec. Heslehurst 4-41	RUASCC 169-6 Loader 34, Walker 29 Sewell 24		Drawn
8 July	H	Southampton University Academic Staff 87 Robinson 7-25	RUASCC 89-5 Sewell 29, Smith 28		Won by 5 wickets
13 July	A	RUASCC 174-9 dec. Ansell 67 Knowlson 27	Bristol University Academicals 169-8 Crabtree 30, Dore 3-53		Drawn
15 July	H	Woodley 114 Giles 4-24	RUASCC 115-8 Knowlson 55		Won by 2 wickets
23 July	H	RUASCC 81 Pearce 29	Abingdon 85-6 Robinson 4-26		Lost by 4 wickets

1971

Captain: A. K. Giles
Vice Captain and Team Secretary: D. J. Ansell
Fixture Secretary: R. J. Loader
Treasurer: R. D. Pearce
Social Member: B. D. Dore

Played 20 Won 4 Lost 7 Drawn 9

Final of Single Wicket Tournament:
M. R. Heslehurst beat R. W. Willey

With the same captain and vice captain as in the previous season and, unusually, no new players able to command a regular place in the side, the results were similar to those in 1970.

Alan Harrison, who suffered a broken nose at Hermitage in 1970, decided (there and then it is said!) not to play again, so Roger Loader took over as Fixture Secretary, a job that Alan had done expertly for five seasons. Bob Pearce became Treasurer.

Bob Willey returned from Australia to lead the bowling averages again and despite an occasional waywardness, Barry Dore was not far behind him. Ansell, Heslehurst and Giles did much of the supporting bowling — which was steady rather than penetrative.

Colin Walker has always been regarded as the batsman in the Club most likely to play an innings of quality without

66

practice — as he often had to. In this season he managed to play 10 innings and topped the averages with 35. Only Max Heslehurst and David Robertson, besides Walker, averaged more than 20 runs an innings. Robertson's 80 against Sussex University Staff, at home, was a superb innings, as was Colin Walker's 85 against David Robertson's Guest XI.

Of the new fixtures (Milton Keynes, Sussex University Staff, St Margaretsbury and Robertson's XI) none were to prove lasting. The wicket that greeted us at Milton Keynes was agricultural to say the least, and the Club struggled hard to muster its record low score of 25. The now traditional matches with Bristol and Southampton Academic Staff sides were high scoring and both drawn. Crabtree scored 85 in an opening stand against us of 203. Facing 212 for 4 at Southampton, the Club responded spiritedly and Giles' 46 not out in 11 scoring strokes was described by Jim Knowlson (who was umpiring at the time) as 'interesting'. There was another exciting draw with Shiplake College, and after our own Students' 1st XI dismissed us for 58 they nearly took their task too lightly, but got home by 2 wickets.

An interesting season — if tinged by the sadness of knowing that Alan Harrison would not be playing for us again. His knowledge of, and enthusiasm for the game, had been of enormous value to a Club finding its feet. His ability is reflected in the statistics in this history — although some of his most splendid moments belonged to the pre-history!

Batting 1971

	Matches	Innings	N. O.	Runs	H. Score	Av.
C. H. Walker	10	10	1	320	85	35.6
M. R. Heslehurst	20	19	6	388	53	29.8
D. H. Robertson	18	18	0	361	80	20.1
D. J. Ansell	12	12	0	207	64	17.2
R. W. Willey	11	8	5	83	48*	16.0
J. R. Knowlson	13	12	3	143	43	15.9
A. K. Giles	19	18	2	218	46*	13.6
W. D. Redfern	18	17	2	190	39	12.7
D. H. S. Foot	13	9	4	55	22	11.0
R. D. Pearce	17	14	1	132	37	10.1
R. J. Loader	16	16	1	112	54	7.5
J. E. Thomas	8	5	1	17	13*	4.2
B. D. Dore	16	6	2	3	2*	0.7

Also batted: A. R. Jones 4, 0; M. J. L. Sangster 3; K. Robinson 4; Owen 1*;
F. G. Stokes 0, 0; N. Caspell 1; C. Ritson 0; F. Robertson 1; N. Caister 0.

Bowling 1971

	Overs	Mdns	Runs	Wkts	Av.	Best
R. W. Willey	110.3	22	356	20	17.8	5-34
B. D. Dore	129	16	402	21	19.1	5-44
D. J. Ansell	83.2	11	312	13	24.0	4-32
J. E. Thomas	57	3	226	9	25.1	4-37
M. R. Heslehurst	89.1	4	369	14	26.4	3-6
A. K. Giles	93	7	383	13	29.5	6-60
A. R. Jones	29.2	1	123	4	30.7	2-19

Also bowled: D. H. Robertson 18-2-71-3; K. Robinson 11-1-21-1;
F. G. Stokes 9-0-41-1; N. Caspell 3-0-9-1; R. D. Pearce 2-0-11-0;
D. Foot 1-0-5-0; N. Caister 11-1-34-5.
Regular Wicket Keeper: J. R. Knowlson

Matches 1971

29 April	A	Wokingham 159-6 dec.	RUASCC 96-7		Drawn
		Ansell 4-13	Ansell 64		
5 May	A	RUASCC 117	Staff College Owls		Lost by
		Walker 40	118-2		8 wickets
9 May	A	Bradfield College 70	RUASCC 71-6		Won by
		Dore 3-12	Redfern 25		4 wickets
		Heslehurst 3-26			
		D. Robertson 3-6			
12 May	A	RUASCC 127-6 dec.	S. M. S. Hermitage		Lost by
		Heslehurst 53	129-3		7 wickets
14 May	H	RUASCC 76-4	Students' 2nd XI		Abandoned
		wickets	did not bat		as a draw
18 May	A	RUASCC 144	Shiplake College		Drawn
		D. Robertson 30	Wanderers 139-9		
		Redfern 39	Giles 6-60		
		Heslehurst 37			
30 May	A	RUASCC 25	Milton Keynes 26-1		Lost by
		(followed by a 20 overs match: lost by 7 runs)			9 wickets
13 June	A	Leckford 157-7 dec.	RUASCC 133-4		Drawn
		Heslehurst 3-29	Knowlson 43		
			Walker 53		
16 June	A	RUASCC 83	Reading School		Lost by
		Ansell 23	All Stars 84-7		3 wickets
			Heslehurst 3-6		
26 June	A	RUASCC 151-7 dec.	Abingdon 146-7		Drawn
		Ansell 34, Walker 37	Ansell 4-32		
		D. Robertson 49			
27 June	H	Students' 2nd XI 143	RUASCC 105-8		Drawn
		Willey 3-28	Knowlson 28		
		Dore 5-44	Walker 25		
29 June	H	RUASCC 58	Students' 1st XI 59-8		Lost by
		Giles 23	Willey 4-14		2 wickets
4 July	A	Sussex University Staff	RUASCC 82		Lost by
		185-5 dec.	D. Robertson 38		103 runs

7 July	A	Southampton University Academic Staff 212-4 dec.	RUASCC 195-5 Loader 54 Robertson 52 Giles 46*	Drawn
8 July	H	RUASCC 123 Heslehurst 34 Redfern 29	St Margaretsbury 124-3	Lost by 7 wickets
11 July	H	D. Robertson's XI 141 Willey 5-34	RUASCC 145-3 Walker 85 Heslehurst 48*	Won by 7 wickets
12 July	H	Bristol University Academicals 203-1 dec. Crabtree 85 Stonebridge 102	RUASCC 157-6 Ansell 41 Heslehurst 39	Drawn
18 July	H	RUASCC 191-9 dec. D. Robertson 80 Heslehurst 31	Sussex University Staff 168-2	Drawn
21 July	A	Woodley 102 Thomas 4-37 Giles 3-17	RUASCC 103-3 D. Robertson 29	Won by 7 wickets
22 July	H	Abingdon 154-7 dec. Caister 5-34	RUASCC 158-5 Heslehurst 48* Walker 48*, Pearce 37	Won by 5 wickets

1972

Captain: D. J. Ansell
Vice Captain: G. E. Dalton
Team: D. H. S. Foot
Fixture Secretary: D. H. Robertson
Treasurer: R. D. Pearce
Social Member: B. D. Dore

Played 26 Won 4 Lost 6 Drawn 16

No Single Wicket Tournament played

This was the first of David Ansell's four consecutive years as captain. A business trip to Botswana made him unavailable for a large part of the season during which the team was led by Vice Captain Graham Dalton as single-minded in his approach to the game — *never* to be lost — as Ansell was relaxed. Twenty-six games were played compared with the usual twenty or so. Winning was still difficult, occasionally, perhaps, (as against LSE) because of Graham Dalton's caution about declaring. New fixtures were played against Surrey University Staff, Caversham, Bluecoat School (all still retained), Cirencester (on tour) and LSE — in due course also to be met in the Sir George Edwards Trophy.

Graham Dalton headed the batting averages and, not for the first time, David Robertson scored most runs. In averaging 24 runs per innings, Mike Sewell after several seasons of modest performance, first began to show the kind of performances subsequently expected from him. His 88 to help draw — and nearly win — the game against Southampton

72

Staff (who had declared at 195 for 4) was his first really big
score; so were Dalton's 85 not out against Wokingham and
his 88 against David Roberton's XI. This was a warm summer
and scores generally began to take on a magnitude that they
had not previously had. In July, on our home wickets, 180
was hardly enough.

When they played together, postgraduate Nick Caistor and
Experimental Officer Carey Hendy could be as formidable an
opening pair as the Club possessed before or since. They were
supported by Dalton, Giles and Jones. Barry Dore now played
less and David Ansell's captaincy made him too reluctant to
bowl himself. Geoff Waites and Alan Robiette had their first
games for the Club and always bowled economically. Brian
Hoskins, although never a regular player, was often to make
valuable contributions, especially as a specialist gully fielder
of the highest quality; and the talented but infrequently
available Howard Dobbs had his first game.

A handsome draw at Wokingham and a good victory at
Leckford — both in May — were rare events. Later in the
season old adversaries Bristol Academicals just held out with
nine wickets down to avoid defeat — thanks mainly (of course)
to Crabtree's 55. The next day (on a two match tour) the Club
did the same at Cirencester — with Knowlson a splendid
number 11 for the occasion! In the final match of the season
there was a sweet victory against Abingdon at Elmhurst Road.
The Club was gradually becoming a more formidable one.

At the A. G. M. at the end of the previous season, Alan Harrison
and Fred Robertson were elected as the Club's first Honorary
Life Members in recognition of their very special contributions
in the early days.

Batting 1972

	Matches	Innings	N. O.	Runs	H. Score	Av.
G. E. Dalton	15	13	1	437	88	36.4
J. R. Knowlson	22	21	8	323	53	24.8
D. H. Robertson	23	23	2	505	71*	24.0
M. J. Sewell	17	17	1	383	88*	23.9
B. J. Hoskins	12	11	3	178	43*	22.2
N. Caistor	13	10	2	156	42	19.5
A. K. Giles	19	18	2	251	54*	15.7
D. J. Ansell	10	9	0	133	35	14.8
R. J. Loader	18	16	5	161	36*	14.6
W. D. Redfern	14	10	3	98	29*	14.0
C. R. C. Hendy	13	10	2	91	27	11.4
C. H. Walker	8	8	0	82	23	10.2
R. D. Pearce	24	19	2	131	32	7.7
B. D. Dore	13	5	3	17	8	8.5

Also batted: H. S. Dobbs 16, 34, 13; D. Griffis 11, 23, 18;
G. M. H. Waites 8, 9, 7; R. Tiwari 6, 15; Murphy 1; Oxborough 3;
Roberts 1, 3*, 1; C. Ritson 3, 0; Bray 8; Hearn 1; Sampson 9; Williams 11.

Bowling 1972

	Overs	Mdns	Runs	Wkts	Av.	Best
N. Caistor	135	24	333	24	13.9	5-26
W. D. Redfern	21	1	86	6	13.3	2-7
G. E. Dalton	118	16	385	21	18.3	4-9
G. M. H. Waites	38	6	113	6	18.8	3-25
C. R. C. Hendy	104	17	343	18	19.0	3-26
B. D. Dore	35	5	149	5	29.8	1-10
A. R. Jones	87	9	341	11	31.0	3-19
Hearn	42	8	153	5	30.6	2-24
A. K. Giles	106	5	506	12	42.2	3-42
D. J. Ansell	36	3	164	3	64.7	2-34

Also bowled: D. H. Robertson 17-0-76-2; A. G. Robiette 17-1-68-5;
Oxborough 10-0-46-2; C. H. Walker 3-0-11-0; R. D. Pearce 1-0-3-0;
Pollock 2-0-6-0; D. H. S. Foot 1-0-2-0; D. Griffis 7-1-30-0.

These averages exclude the match against LSE when Hendy took 5 wickets,
Giles 2, and Jones 1.
Regular Wicket Keeper: J. R. Knowlson

Matches 1972

3 May	A	Minley Manor 114 Caistor 5-26 Giles 4-48	RUASCC 79 Giles 25	Lost by 35 runs
13 May	H	RUASCC 145-7 dec. Giles 50* Robertson 30	Students' 2nd XI 112-3	Drawn
16 May	A	RUASCC 136 Sewell 36 Robertson 28 Knowlson 25	Shiplake College Wanderers 92-7 Hendy 3-32	Drawn
17 May	A	RUASCC 185-4 dec. Dalton 85*	Wokingham 131-2	Drawn
25 May	A	Reading School All Stars 131-5 dec.	RUASCC 134-4 Giles 27 Knowlson 53	Won by 6 wickets
27 May	H	Leckford 44 Dalton 4-9	RUASCC 45-2 Knowlson 18	Won by 8 wickets
28 May	H	Milton Keynes 113-7 Hendy 3-33	RUASCC 71 Pearce 22	Lost by 42 runs
31 May	A	East Tytherley 160-6 dec. Hendy 3-50	RUASCC 87-9 Foot 26	Drawn
4 June	A	RUASCC 166-6 dec. Robertson 71 Sewell 35	Surrey University Staff	Abandoned as a draw
6 June	A	RUASCC 120-7 dec. Robertson 46	Bluecoat School 121-7 Giles 3-42	Lost by 3 wickets
7 June	H	RUASCC 151-5 dec. Sewell 48 Robertson 47	L. S. E. 105-8	Drawn
11 June	A	RUASCC 89-9 dec. Knowlson 28	Leckford 60-7 Waites 3-25 Jones 3-19	Drawn

14 June	A	RUASCC 148 Dalton 70	Reading School All Stars 152-9 Dalton 3-26	Lost by 1 wicket
17 June	A	Caversham 157-8 dec. Giles 4-33 Dalton 3-42	RUASCC 103-5 Dobbs 34	Drawn
21 June	A	RUASCC 150 Dalton 49 Ansell 30	S. M. S. Hermitage 151-2	Lost by 8 wickets
		RUASCC 108 Hoskins 23 Wilson 9-32	Students' 1st XI 10-1	Abandoned as a draw
29 June	A	RUASCC 122 Robertson 40 Redfern 29	Abingdon 124-2	Lost by 8 wickets
5 July	H	Southampton University Academic Staff 195-4 dec.	RUASCC 191-6 Sewell 88 Redfern 29	Drawn
6 July	H	St Margaretsbury 170-7 dec.	RUASCC 120-7 Hoskins 43*	Drawn
9 July	A	Sussex University Staff 145-5 dec. Caistor 3-30	RUASCC 107-6 Dalton 59	Drawn
11 July	A	RUASCC 141-7 dec. Sewell 33	Bristol University Academicals 128-9 Crabtree 55 Caistor 4-33	Drawn
12 July	A	Cirencester 160-6 dec. Dalton 2-16	RUASCC 139-9 Ansell 35, Sewell 28 Webb 8-65	Drawn
16 July	H	D. Robertson's XI 164-7 dec. Robiette 3-40 Hendy 3-26	RUASCC 175-1 Dalton 88 Knowlson 49	Won by 9 wickets

19 July	H	RUASCC 178-5 dec. Giles 54* Robertson 50	Woodley 132-5 Caistor 3-33	Drawn
23 July	H	RUASCC 183-7 dec. Dalton 85 Loader 34	Sussex University Staff 172-8	Drawn
27 July	H	Abingdon 179-6 dec.	RUASCC 180-7 Loader 36* Pearce 32	Won by 3 wickets

Against the Students' 1st XI, 1974

Standing (left to right) Alan Harrison (Umpire), Bob Willey, Alec Jones, Mike Sewell, Carey Hendy, Bob Pearce (Scorer), Roger Loader, Wally Redfern

Seated (left to right) David Robertson, Graham Dalton, David Ansell, Tony Giles, Jim Knowlson.

Leighton Park, 1978

Budd in full flow

Redfern loses his bails

Biddiss at full stretch

Sewell in stubborn mood

Club photograph, 1978

Standing (left to right) Roger Smith, Dai Edwards, Mike Pursglove, Peter Fitzgerald, George Norman, Bob Pearce, Alan Robiette, Peter Crane, Jim Knowlson, Joe Gartner, Roger Loader, Steve Adkins, Dave Petherick.
Seated (left to right) Richard Tranter, Tony Giles, Mike Sewell, Graham Crampton, Mike Butler.

Waiting for tea , Leighton Park , 1978

Ansell with head down

Tranter digs one out

RUASCC at Abingdon, 1982
Standing (left to right) M. J. Sewell, F. Tallett, T. Ridley, I. Warburton, J. Budd, R. B. Tranter.
Kneeling (left to right) D. M. Pursglove, D. J. Ansell, C. Miles, G. R. Crampton, P. M. Hotten.

Batting at Whitchurch (Hants)

Leighton Park, 1978

Dalton's cap. Graham Dalton threw this cap into the Club's gear bag after his last game for the Club before leaving for Aberdeen early in the 1976 season. It remained there, as our most treasured artifact, until, guesting for the Club in 1982, Graham took it back to Scotland with him. Originally it was not his — but belonged to one W. Derby, a Methodist preacher and wily old leg spinner who played for Calver Cricket Club, in Derbyshire. He gave his cap to young Dalton when he retired from the game — so presumably it's back where it belongs — but we miss it!

The Sir George Edwards Trophy

1973

Captain: D. J. Ansell
Vice Captain and Team Secretary: G. E. Dalton
Fixture Secretary: D. H. Robertson
Treasurer: R. D. Pearce
Social Member: J. R. Knowlson

Played 23 Won 6 Lost 6 Drawn 11

Final of Single Wicket Tournament:
G. E. Dalton beat R. W. Willey

David Ansell's second season as captain, with an unchanged
team of 'officials' to support him, except that Knowlson took
over from Barry Dore who had been social member for several
years and had now hung up his boots. By contrast Keith
Robinson, after injury in 1972, took his out again and with
Bob Willey, partially recovered from a back injury, Graham
Dalton and Carey Hendy made up a formidable attack.
Against Leckford, Willey and Robinson bowled unchanged
and gave the Club an easy victory.

No new players arrived to play regularly, but the name of
P. Fitzgerald appears for the first time — amongst 'also bowled'.
For the first time Jim Knowlson topped the batting averages,
well supported by Graham Dalton, Mike Sewell, David Robertson
and Carey Hendy (no mere fast bowler).

There were five new fixtures — three of them still appearing
each year on the list: Royal Ascot, Bramshill Police College and

Mandarins. Dismissed for 109 in the second match of the season by Royal Ascot, the side bowled and fielded well to win by 20 runs — Dalton giving a fine all round performance.

There were other highlights — victory at home against Bristol Academicals — for the first time since the fixture began in 1961. Crabtree this time being restricted to a mere 12. In a closely drawn game against Bluecoat School, Bob Pearce played a remarkable innings of 37. He simply went berserk. He had often threatened to, but this time hit the jackpot!

The heavy beating at Wokingham in May was something that we were going to have to get used to. Graham Dalton, without doubt our most powerful all rounder ever, won the Single Wicket Trophy.

Batting 1973

	Matches	Innings	N. O.	Runs	H. Score	Av.
J. R. Knowlson	15	13	3	307	86*	30.7
G. E. Dalton	16	16	3	364	52*	28.0
D. H. Robertson	13	12	3	219	47	24.3
M. J. Sewell	20	20	0	472	57	23.6
C. R. C. Hendy	17	14	2	243	44*	20.2
H. S. Dobbs	11	10	1	143	33	15.9
D. Robins	14	13	6	110	26	15.7
D. J. Ansell	17	15	1	211	52	15.1
R. D. Pearce	21	18	2	225	37	14.1
W. D. Redfern	12	10	1	126	34	14.0
R. J. Loader	17	14	3	151	52*	13.7
A. K. Giles	14	13	0	144	40	11.1
M. Turner	11	9	2	50	25	7.1

Also batted: D. Griffis 52; A. Robinson 48; C. H. Walker 13, 44*, 12, 20;
R. W. Willey 17, 0, 1, 55; A. Smithson 1, 7*; K. Robinson 6, 4;
A. G. Robiette 9, 1, 3; A. R. Jones 0, 2*, 0*; B. Rawlings 2, 0; J. Phippen 1;
Howe 0; P. Rawlinson 0; R. Speddy 0.

Bowling 1973

	Overs	Mdns	Runs	Wkts	Av.	Best
R. W. Willey	93.5	22	232	16	14.5	4-11
G. E. Dalton	153.0	20	547	34	16.1	5-42
H. S. Dobbs	33.0	0	192	11	17.4	5-33
K. Robinson	95.0	14	359	20	17.9	6-34
A. G. Robiette	48.0	11	154	9	18.1	3-18
C. R. C. Hendy	165.5	27	608	30	20.3	5-43
A. K. Giles	80.0	9	359	11	32.6	3-39
D. J. Ansell	72.5	9	278	8	34.7	2-15
M. Turner	21.0	1	105	2	52.5	1-35
A. R. Jones	42.0	8	176	3	58.7	1-10

Also bowled: R. Speddy 6-0-16-1; D. Griffis 11-3-44-2;
M. J. Sewell 15-1-70-3; P. Fitzgerald 13-0-72-2; D. H. Robertson 5-0-24-0;
A. Smithson 8-0-55-0
Regular Wicket Keeper: J. R. Knowlson

Matches 1973

Date		Home/Away	Team 1	Team 2	Result
2 May	A	RUASCC 162-8 dec. Ansell 52 Knowlson 41 Dobbs 26	Staff College Owls 163-7 Hendy 5-54	Lost by 3 wickets
9 May	A	RUASCC 109 Dalton 28	Royal Ascot 89 Dalton 3-19	Won by 20 runs
13 May	H	RUASCC 176-7 dec. Sewell 53 Knowlson 29 Ansell 28, Dobbs 24	Students' 2nd XI 165-5 Willey 3-50	Drawn
15 May	A	RUASCC 157-9 dec. Griffith 52 Knowlson 36 Robins 26	Shiplake College Wanderers 152-9	Drawn
16 May	A	Wokingham 207-4 dec.	RUASCC 81 Sewell 39, Redfern 22	Lost by 126 runs
20 May	A	RUASCC 134 Sewell 46 Giles 40	Bearwood College Staff 93-8 Giles 3-39	Drawn
27 May	H	Milton Keynes 146 Hendy 5-43 K. Robinson 3-60	RUASCC 147-7 A. Robinson 48 Hendy 34	Won by 3 wickets
3 June	A	RUASCC 167-8 dec. Redfern 34 Dobbs 33	Surrey 167-4	Drawn
5 June	A	RUASCC 181-6 dec. Walker 44* Pearce 37, Ansell 33	Bluecoat School 179-5	Drawn
6 June	A	RUASCC 205-6 dec. Sewell 57, Ansell 39 Loader 33, Turner 25	L. S. E. 142-6 Gillingham 83*	Drawn

13 June	A	RUASCC 142 Willey 55 Sewell 24	Reading School All Stars 119 Willey 4-11 Robiette 3-18	Won by 23 runs
17 June	A	Leckford 66 Robinson 6-34 Willey 4-31	RUASCC 67-2 Sewell 21 Knowlson 19	Won by 8 wickets
27 June	A	Bramshill Police College 154-9 Dalton 3-39	RUASCC 54-3 Dalton 41*	Drawn
3 July	H	RUASCC 158-7 dec. Sewell 38 D. Robertson 34* Dalton 33	Students' 1st XI 161-1 Blease 81* Goldberg 53*	Lost by 9 wickets
8 July	A	Sussex University Staff 171-9 dec. Robinson 4-33	RUASCC 101 Sewell 27, Dalton 19 Hendy 18	Lost by 70 runs
10 July	H	Bristol University Academicals 116 Hendy 4-29, Dalton 4-30	RUASCC 117-5 Loader 52* Sewell 29	Won by 5 wickets
11 July	A	Cirencester 215-2 dec. Webb 104* Frape 93	RUASCC 119-8 D. Robertson 32 Hendy 24	Drawn
14 July	H	Mandarins 133 Dobbs 3-24	RUASCC 135-4 D. Robertson 47 Knowlson 35* Dalton 32	Won by 6 wickets
18 July	A	Southampton University Academic Staff 166-9 dec. Dalton 5-74	RUASCC 126 Hendy 31* Sewell 23	Lost by 40 runs
22 July	H	RUASCC 186-8 dec. Dalton 39 D. Robertson 38 Redfern 34	Sussex University Staff 170-7 Sewell 3-70	Drawn

25 July	A	Woodley 202-7 dec.	RUASCC 160-8	Drawn
		Dalton 5-42	Dalton 44, Hendy 31	
			Redfern 28	
11 Aug.	H	RUASCC 186-5 dec.	Mandarins 114-9	Drawn
		Knowlson 86*	Dobbs 5-33	
		Hendy 44*	Dalton 3-23	
		D. Robertson 25		
19 Aug.	H	Allen & Unwin	RUASCC 176	Lost by
		189-7 dec.	Dalton 52 ret. to	13 runs
		Dalton 3-43	preach!	
			Sewell 26	

1974

Captain: D. J. Ansell
Vice Captain and Team Secretary: G. E. Dalton
Fixture Secretary: D. H. Robertson
Treasurer: R. D. Pearce
Social Member: J. R. Knowlson

Played 29 Won 10 Lost 10 Drawn 8 Tied 1

Final of Single Wicket Tournament:
C. H. Walker beat R. W. Willey

David Ansell's third year of captaincy. After ten seasons when
the number of games played varied between 14 and 26 (usually
in the low twenties) 29 games were played. This was a significant jump forward, with matches for the first time being
played in August. Of five new fixtures, three still remain on
the list: the Students' 3rd XI, Bluecoat School and Reading
Lawyers. Ten games were won, three more than in any previous season and the game with Leckford was the third to be
tied in the Club's history. No new star players burst onto the
scene, but Mike Pursglove played in a third of the fixtures,
and remains a valuable administrator and player. Richard
Tranter guested for one game.

Jim Knowlson topped the batting averages for the second
successive year followed closely by the rapidly improving
Mike Sewell and by David Robertson, playing in his last full
season before moving to Australia. A revitalised Keith
Robinson was at the top of the regular bowlers' averages,
bowling more overs (138) than ever before, with the exception

86

of 1970 (162). Robinson, Dalton, Hendy, Giles, Willey and Ansell constituted the regular bowling attack in that order of overs bowled. Carey Hendy on his day was a formidable bowler, and his 8 for 33 at S. M. S. Hermitage brought about a 6 run victory.

The side was especially pleased to draw at Royal Ascot after being 36 for 7, facing 140 — thanks to stubborn resistance from Dalton (who hit one huge six), Willey and a late order Knowlson; and losing to Wokingham by only 17 runs was almost hailed as a victory! Another pleasing performance was the 69 for 2 against the Students' 1st XI's total of 137 for 8, before rain stopped play. Who knows?! The most salutary lesson, however, came against Christ Church College, who were left very little time to reach the 116 that the Club had crawled to, while losing 8 wickets against an attack that was a yard or two faster than our normal opponents. The college openers got them without loss and with twenty minutes to spare!

A low scoring game was lost at Bristol, with Crabtree (who else?) scoring 49. Rain the next day prevented any play against Cardiff University staff — but the evening out in Bristol had its moments.

Batting 1974

	Matches	Innings	N. O.	Runs	H. Score	Av.
J. R. Knowlson	19	19	6	405	53	31.1
M. J. Sewell	21	21	1	569	77	28.4
D. H. Robertson	26	26	4	531	51	24.1
D. J. Ansell	24	22	2	388	50	19.4
G. E. Dalton	18	15	1	231	39	16.5
A. K. Giles	21	17	2	243	45	16.2
R. W. Willey	10	9	2	85	33	12.1
R. D. Pearce	22	20	2	197	40	10.9
C. R. C. Hendy	14	12	1	101	23	9.2
C. H. Walker	8	8	0	69	30	8.6
D. E. Penny	18	15	3	102	24	8.5
D. M. Pursglove	12	6	3	23	12*	7.7
W. D. Redfern	16	14	1	97	21	7.5
A. G.Robiette	12	10	2	55	15	6.9
R. J. Loader	21	16	2	91	28	6.1
A. R. Jones	8	4	1	13	13	4.3
K. Robinson	15	10	6	6	2	1.5

Also batted: H. S. Dobbs 0, 21*, 49*; D. Griffis 39; Hansen 15;
F. Robertson 11, 2; Raj Dubey 6*, 3, 9; Townsend 8; T. E. Josling 14, 1;
D. H. S. Foot 1, 2, 10; F. Eggleton 3; R. B. Tranter 3; Sanghera 0;
B. J. Hoskins 0, 0; Skretkowicz 0*; C. Ritson 1*, 1*.

Bowling 1974

	Overs	Mdns	Runs	Wkts	Av.	Best
D. H. Robertson	38.2	7	162	15	10.8	4-5
K. Robinson	138.5	23	418	32	13.1	5-25
D. E. Penny	31.2	0	170	12	14.2	4-44
A. R. Jones	29	4	114	8	14.2	3-6
G. E. Dalton	161.5	23	527	33	16.0	4-20
R. W. Willey	96.2	23	247	15	16.5	4-10
A. K. Giles	109.4	11	373	22	16.9	3-29
D. M. Pursglove	59	1	295	17	17.3	4-36
C. R. C. Hendy	119	21	369	21	17.6	8-33
D. J. Ansell	90.5	15	265	15	17.7	4-24
A. G. Robiette	50	3	213	3	71.0	1-14

Also bowled: D. Griffis 7-1-12-2; Townshend 5-2-7-1;
R. B. Tranter 14-1-40-5; H. S. Dobbs 8-0-53-2; P. Fitzgerald 10-0-67-2;
Hansen 5-2-11-0; F. Eggleton 4-0-35-0.
Regular Wicket Keeper: J. R. Knowlson

Matches 1974

Date		Team / Scores	Opponent / Scores	Result
1 May	A	RUASCC 125-8 dec. Sewell 65* Loader 27	Staff College Owls 128-6	Lost by 4 wickets
5 May	H	Students' 3rd XI 82 Ansell 4-24	RUASCC 85-4 Robertson 47*	Won by 6 wickets
8 May	A	Royal Ascot 140-8 dec.	RUASCC 82-8	Drawn
12 May	H	RUASCC 150-8 dec. Giles 45, Pearce 34*	Students' 2nd XI 151-4	Lost by 6 wickets
15 May	H	Wokingham 188-8 dec. Pursglove 4-70	RUASCC 171 Ansell 28, Loader 28	Lost by 17 runs
16 May	H	RUASCC 163-4 dec. Ansell 45, Giles 42* Dalton 27, Sewell 25	Employees 71-9 Penny 3-10	Drawn
18 May	A	RUASCC 132 Sewell 40, Ansell 30 Walker 30	Green Park 70 Robinson 5-25 Dalton 3-5	Won by 62 runs
21 May	A	RUASCC 166-9 dec. Sewell 72 Robertson 25	Shiplake College Wanderers 102 Robinson 4-19 Penny 4-44	Won by 64 runs
22 May	A	RUASCC 112 Ansell 35, Pearce 26	S. M. S. Hermitage 106 Hendy 8-33	Won by 6 runs
29 May	A	RUASCC 112 Ansell 35 Lewis 6-49	L. S. E. 115-5 Pursglove 3-31 Josling 68*	Lost by 5 wickets
30 May	A	Reading School 155-8 dec. Willey 3-24 Robinson 3-41	RUASCC 129-6 Dalton 39 Knowlson 34*	Drawn
3 June	H	Surrey University Staff 198-7 dec.	RUASCC 200-5 Sewell 77 Robertson 46 Giles 26*	Won by 5 wickets

4 June	A	Bluecoat School 141-8 dec. Jones 3-22	RUASCC 82-7	Drawn
5 June	A	RUASCC 102 Robertson 37 Ansell 27	Wokingham 105-5 Giles 3-36	Lost by 5 wickets
9 June	A	RUASCC 116-8 dec. Robertson 42* Willey 33	Christ Church College 117-0	Lost by 10 wickets
12 June	A	RUASCC 155 Ansell 50 Dalton 28	Reading School All Stars 158-5	Lost by 5 wickets
13 June	H	Employees 112-6	RUASCC 114-8 Knowlson 53	Won by 2 wickets (limited overs)
16 June	A	Leckford 92 Jones 3-6	RUASCC 92 Hicks 6-40	Tied
19 June	A	RUASCC 125 Robertson 51	S. M. S. Hermitage 94-9 Dalton 4-20, Giles 3-29	Drawn
27 June	H	Abingdon 86-8 dec.	RUASCC 88-3 Sewell 36	Won by 7 wickets
29 June	H	RUASCC 161-4 dec. Sewell 65 Knowlson 50 Robertson 30	Lawyers 153-6 Ansell 2-29	Drawn
2 July	H	Students' 1st XI 137-8 dec. Dalton 3-38	RUASCC 69-2 Knowlson 28* Ansell 25*	Drawn
3 July	H	RUASCC 158 Robertson 46 Dalton 33	Bramshill Police College 161-8 Dalton 3-37 Hendy 3-58	Lost by 2 wickets
9 July	A	RUASCC 94 Robertson 34	Bristol University Academicals 95-7 Dalton 3-29	Lost by 3 wickets

14 July	H	RUASCC 118-9 dec.	Mandarins 119-7	Lost by
		Knowlson 32	Robinson 3-33	3 wickets
17 July	H	Southampton	RUASCC 119-8	Drawn
		University Academic	Knowlson 51	
		Staff 163-9 dec.	Pearce 40	
		Gardner 101		
		Tranter 5-40		
19 July	H	RUASCC 133-9 dec.	Postgraduates 100	Won by
		Robertson 41	Robertson 4-15	33 runs
			Robinson 4-21	
28 July	H	Allen & Unwin 133	RUASCC 134-9	Won by
		Willey 4-10	Griffis 39	1 wicket
		Giles 3-37	Robertson 26	
10 Aug.	H	Mandarins 133	RUASCC 135-3	Won by
		Pursglove 4-36	Sewell 54	7 wickets
		Dalton 3-31	Dobbs 49*	
		Robertson 3-31		

1975

Captain: D. J. Ansell
Vice Captain: G. E. Dalton
Team Secretary: R. J. Loader
Fixture Secretary: D. H. Robertson
Treasurer: R. D. Pearce
Social Member: J. R. Knowlson

Played 34 Won 12 Lost 13 Drawn 9

No Single Wicket Tournament played

David Ansell created a record by captaining the side for the
fourth consecutive season. With another increase in the number
of games played (to 34) and names like Petherick, Tranter and
Butler appearing, the Club was gradually moving towards the
one that exists at the time of writing. David Robertson and
Graham Dalton played their last season for the Club and
Keith Robinson his last complete season. It would be hard to
imagine the side without them; each in his own way had been
a tower of strength.

With so many conventional fixtures, the Single Wicket
Tournament was not played. A new venture, however, was the
Sir George Edwards Trophy contested for at Surrey University
by four University Staff sides. Disappointingly, RUASCC lost
both its games, against Surrey and Southampton, and became
the first holders of the wooden spoon.

93

New fixtures were played against Stoke Row and Checkendon.
After a wet start to the season, a very warm July and August
meant that 200 runs per innings were the norm at Elmhurst
Road. Several victories were won chasing high scores — including
Reading Lawyers 213 for 1 (Messenger 100 not out),
Checkendon's 199 and Mandarins 214 for 8 — thanks to a
reliability of the batting (from Knowlson, Sewell, Dalton, Ansell,
Butler and Heslehurst) that had not previously been seen. Max
Heslehurst on a second short visit from Queensland was a much
improved batsman and was the first Club member to score a
century (124 not out against the Mandarins). Humberstone
(guesting from St Margaretsbury) scored another one — but a
century still eluded a 'home produced' batsman. Twice in the
season Graham Dalton reached the nineties and his 97 against
Reading School All Stars was especially punishing.

A five wicket win at Abingdon and a nine wicket win over
Bramshill were rare victories in the history of those two
fixtures, and were two of the 21 games which the Club either
won or drew. A good season, with unquestionably the
strongest team the Club had yet fielded: a blend of the old
and the new, with Keith Robinson bowling more overs than
ever before (taking 5 wickets per innings in four consecutive
games) and David Petherick taking over where Carey Hendy
had left off.

Batting 1975

	Matches	Innings	N. O.	Runs	H. Score	Av.
M. D. S. Butler	13	12	6	307	75	51.2
G. E. Dalton	20	16	1	558	97	37.2
R. B. Tranter	10	9	3	211	63	35.2
M. R. Heslehurst	18	17	2	499	124*	33.3
J. R. Knowlson	24	21	2	562	67	29.6
M. J. Sewell	19	18	1	496	64	29.2
D. J. Ansell	24	22	1	535	74	25.5
D. M. Pursglove	21	8	7	22	6*	22.0
C. H. Walker	5	5	1	85	41	21.2
D. H. Robertson	5	5	2	47	29	15.7
A. K. Giles	22	21	3	254	41*	14.1
C. Hemmings	21	14	3	138	34	12.5
R. J. Loader	22	19	2	211	50	12.4
R. D. Pearce	23	20	4	167	42*	10.4
D. E. Penny	18	12	3	82	18*	9.1
W. D. Redfern	10	7	0	33	14	4.7
A. G. Robiette	10	6	1	19	9	3.8
D. J. Petherick	19	7	2	17	8	3.4
K. Robinson	20	6	2	11	5	2.7

Also batted: J. Humberstone (guest) 101; T. E. Josling 37*, 10, 1*, 0;
C. R. C. Hendy 7, 5*, 16; Ellis Jones 10, 9; A. R. Jones 5, 1;
W. Straker-Nesbit (student) 6; P. Rawlinson 4; C. Ritson 1, 0*, 0*;
J. A. Giles (guest) 0.

Bowling 1975

	Overs	Mdns	Runs	Wkts	Av.	Best
C. R. C. Hendy	29	10	65	10	6.5	4-14
K. Robinson	211.3	37	683	43	15.9	5-20
R. B. Tranter	99	15	400	24	16.7	4-24
G. E. Dalton	182	24	585	33	17.7	4-16
D. M. Pursglove	58.1	2	276	15	18.4	5-40
P. J. Petherick	132.2	19	496	24	20.7	6-25
A. G. Robiette	36.3	2	175	7	25.0	4-27
A. K. Giles	126.5	15	609	24	25.4	8-43
M. R. Heslehurst	61	8	244	9	27.1	3-24
A. R. Jones	95	17	354	13	27.2	2-19
D. J. Ansell	122	15	492	17	28.9	3-27

Also bowled: M. J. Sewell 12-1-60-6; J. R. Knowlson 16-5-76-6;
C. Ritson 3-1-17-1; D. H. Robertson 5-0-37-1; D. Griffis 14-1-53-1;
Ellis-Jones 13-1-60-1; C. Hemmings 4-0-35-0; J. Humberstone 3-0-20-0.
Regular Wicket Keeper: J. R. Knowlson

Matches 1975

26 April	H	RUASCC 62 Sewell 14	Caversham 66-3	Lost by 7 wickets
30 April	A	Staff College Owls 68-7 dec. Dalton 3-13 Petherick 3-16		Abandoned as a draw
4 May	H	RUASCC 172-7 dec. Sewell 172-7 Ansell 43, Giles 27	Students' 3rd XI 167-8	Drawn
7 May	A	Royal Ascot C. C. 53-2		Abandoned as a draw
11 May	H	RUASCC 130 Knowlson 58	Students' 2nd XI 94 Hendy 4-27 Robinson 3-17 Dalton 3-41	Won by 36 runs
14 May	A	Wokingham 189-7 dec. Dalton 4-41	RUASCC 134 Ansell 32, Sewell 25	Lost by 55 runs
17 May	H	Employees 79 Sewell 3-9 Robinson 3-17 Heslehurst 3-24	RUASCC 80-3 Josling 37*	Won by 7 wickets
21 May	A	RUASCC 161-4 dec. Knowlson 51* Ansell 49 Robertson 29	S. M. S. Hermitage 162-9 Pursglove 3-23	Lost by 1 wicket
28 May	A	RUASCC 178-5 dec. Dalton 91 Heslehurst 44	L. S. E. 118-4	Drawn
31 May	A	RUASCC 170-9 dec. Dalton 68 Ansell 33 Sewell 32	Reading School All Stars 108 Pursglove 5-40 Knowlson 3-15	Won by 62 runs

1 June	H	RUASCC 210-6 dec. Butler 75 Knowlson 67	Surrey University Staff 159 Giles 8-43	Won by 51 runs
3 June	A	Bluecoat School 144-6 dec.	RUASCC 145-3	Won by 7 wickets
4 June	A	RUASCC 134-5 dec. Sewell 55 Dalton 35	Bramshill Police College 69-7 Dalton 4-16	Drawn
8 June	A	Christ Church College 112 Dalton 4-28 Petherick 3-49	RUASCC 87 Ansell 34 Dalton 21 Chitty 8-34	Lost by 25 runs
11 June	A	RUASCC 178-7 dec. Dalton 97 Pearce 30	Reading School All Stars 179-3	Lost by 7 wickets
15 June	A	RUASCC 190-8 dec. Heslehurst 87 Sewell 35 Walker 22	Leckford 159-6 Robinson 5-53	Drawn
19 June	H	Employees 95-8 Robinson 5-20	RUASCC 98-3 Ansell 28, Butler 26* Sewell 22*	Won by 7 wickets (limited overs)
22 June	A	Green Park 105 Robinson 5-22	RUASCC 89 Sewell 30	Lost by 16 runs
27 June	A	Abingdon 128-9 dec. Robinson 5-51	RUASCC 132-5 Hemmings 34 Heslehurst 31 Knowlson 21	Won by 5 wickets
28 June	H	Reading Lawyers 213-1 dec. Messenger 100* Aram 86*	RUASCC 214-5 Heslehurst 66 Sewell 64, Dalton 30 Butler 21*	Won by 5 wickets
1 July	H	Students' 1st XI 200-8 dec. Dalton 3-58	RUASCC 157-4 Dalton 63, Butler 33* Hemmings 26*	Drawn

2 July	H	Bramshill Police	RUASCC 83-1	Won by
		College 81	Pearce 42*	9 wickets
		Petherick 6-25	Loader 24	
		Ansell 3-27		
5 July	H	Checkendon 199	RUASCC 200-7	Won by
		Powell 92	Butler 63*	3 wickets
		Robinson 5-55	Heslehurst 45	
		Petherick 3-65	Pearce 31	
6 July	A	RUASCC 67	Shiplake College	Lost by
		Ansell 19	Wanderers 70-4	6 wickets
		Loader 17		
9 July	H	RUASCC 197-8 dec.	Reading Lawyers	Drawn
		Ansell 45, Tranter 43*	116-8	
		Sewell 32	Tranter 4-30	
		Heslehurst 31		
13 July	H	Mandarins 214-8 dec.	RUASCC 215-2	Won by
		Mayhew 100*	Heslehurst 124*	8 wickets
			Dalton 54*, Sewell 26	

Sir George Edwards Trophy: First Round (limited overs)

16 July	A	Surrey University	RUASCC 182-9	Lost by
		Staff 229	Knowlson 62	47 runs
		Dalton 3-27	Giles 32	
		Tranter 3-47		

Sir George Edwards Trophy: Loser's Tie (limited overs)

17 July	A	Southampton	RUASCC 154-9	Lost by
		University Staff 181-9	Ansell 74	27 runs
		Tranter 4-24	Tranter 25	
23 July	H	RUASCC 236-7 dec.	Woodley 204-6	Drawn
		Ansell 69, Dalton 55	Mountjoy 84*	
		Walker 41	Tranter 4-57	
		Heslehurst 34		
27 July	H	RUASCC 214-4 dec.	Allen & Unwin 215-2	Lost by
		Humberstone 101	Stevenson 110	8 wickets
		Butler 44*, Ansell 43	Anderson 80*	
9 Aug.	H	RUASCC 195-8 dec.	Mandarins 196-2	Lost by
		Tranter 63	Mayhew 80*	8 wickets
		Loader 50	Hadley 73*	
			Robinson 2-69	

13 Aug.	H	Royal Ascot	RUASCC 95	Lost by
		209-8 dec.	Loader 29	114 runs
		Bassett 76		
		Robiette 4-27		
17 Aug.	H	Stoke Row 98	RUASCC 99-7	Won by
		Hendy 4-14	Tranter 28*	3 wickets
		Tranter 3-24	Knowlson 28	
31 Aug.	A	RUASCC 130-5 dec.	Caversham 131-3	Lost by
		Knowlson 56*		7 wickets
		Giles 41*		

1976

Captain: J. R. Knowlson
Vice Captain: A. K. Giles
Team Secretary: R. J. Loader
Fixture Secretary: M. J. Sewell
Treasurer: R. D. Pearce

Played 39 Won 13 Lost 16 Drawn 10

**Final of the last Single Wicket Tournament:
D. J. Ansell beat D. Edwards**

Jim Knowlson began the first of his two years as captain with an encouraging draw against Caversham, victory over the Owls and a draw against the Students' 3rd XI. The number of games played reached a new 'high' with the enthusiastic Mike Sewell now making the fixtures. Thirteen victories were recorded — one more than the previous record. The sixteen defeats included games against all four new opponents: Wokingham Schoolmasters, West Ilsley, Mapledurham and Hurst.

For the first time in the Club's history, three batsmen scored more than 500 runs: Sewell (755), Ansell (670) and Knowlson (509) whilst Roger Loader had easily his best season to date, averaging nearly 20. These four helped to compensate for the loss of Graham Dalton who left for Aberdeen after two games and Mike Butler who, apart from 5 games, elected for a season with Reading C. C. David Ansell's 102 against Allen & Unwin was the first century by a regular member of the Club and his 79 against Mapledurham was thought by those who saw it to be one of the best innings ever played for the Club. David also became the second player to win the Single Wicket Tournament twice, beating newcomer Dai Edwards in the final. The brunt of the attack was borne by David Petherick who bowled more than twice as many overs (293) than in the previous season and took 61 wickets for less than 16 apiece. His nearest rivals were Ansell and Giles with 36 and 28 wickets respectively. Richard Tranter's all round performances helped to compensate for the loss of Graham Dalton.

With so many fixtures, a larger than usual number of players were called upon and valuable newcomers included Graham Crampton (to become one of our very best team secretaries) Dave Smith and Dave Robeson. Amongst 'also batted and bowled' the names of George Norman, Peter Crane, Andy Baum and Dave Bannister appeared once or twice — all to appear more often in subsequent seasons.

Outstanding victories were recorded (for the first time ever) against Caversham, dismissed largely by Petherick and Tranter for 41, and against the School of Military Survey who fell short of the Club's laboured 100 for 8 by 10 runs.

Some good performances were also recorded in games that were lost. For the Students' 1st XI Yates's 9 for 32 always had the Club struggling, but it cost the students 5 wickets to pass the required 101. After a good win against L. S. E. in the first round of the Sir George Edwards Trophy (Knowlson 78 not out) a score of 201 was not enough against the Surrey Staff, despite a hostile spell from Petherick reducing them, at first, to 34 for 4. And even 211 for 6 against Wokingham was not enough to avoid defeat.

But it was a good season — in the heat and hard grounds of the famous drought year. Jim Knowlson brought his experience as a captain and his stubbornness as an opening bat to his job as captain. His vice captain added to the general feeling of experience at the helm.

Batting 1976

	Matches	Innings	N. O.	Runs	H. Score	Av.
M. J. Sewell	25	25	4	755	86*	36.0
J. R. Knowlson	25	21	4	509	78*	29.9
D. J. Ansell	26	24	1	670	102	29.1
M. D. S. Butler	5	5	-	137	57	27.4
A. K. Giles	19	16	6	244	58*	24.4
R. J. Loader	27	25	1	475	67	19.8
R. D. Pearce	27	21	5	290	41*	18.1
R. B. Tranter	15	14	2	198	47	16.5
D. J. Petherick	30	19	6	206	38*	15.8
D. J. Smith	23	20	3	252	61	14.8
D. G. Hay	8	8	2	81	29*	13.5
K. Robinson	13	5	3	24	10	12.0
G. R. Crampton	28	28	3	292	47	11.7
D. Edwards	8	8	-	76	19	9.5
P. Wright	20	15	2	109	23	8.4
D. Robeson	28	22	7	124	27	8.3
D. Russell	9	7	1	48	17	8.0
P. J. Giddings	11	8	2	47	11	7.8
W. D. Redfern	8	8	-	61	31	7.6
P. Fitzgerald	10	6	3	12	4*	4.0
D. M. Pursglove	22	11	2	35	11	3.9

Also batted: H. S. Dobbs 31*; G. E. Dalton 22*, 52; Thomas 70; Grayson 19;
J. A. Giles 18; B. J. Hoskins 25, 7, 7; D. J. Bannister 7, 4, 22;
W. Straker-Nesbit 6; Disney 5*, 0, 0*; F. Robertson 4, 1; R. Warriner 0, 3;
C. Nixon (student) 1; A. E. Baum 0; P. R. Corner 0; D. Holland 0;
A. Cowling 0, 0; C. Ritson 0.

Bowling 1976

	Overs	Mdns	Runs	Wkts	Av.	Best
D. J. Petherick	293	53	953	61	15.6	6-28
P. J. Giddings	59.4	6	226	13	17.4	3-15
J. R. Knowlson	77.2	3	394	21	18.7	5-47
D. J. Ansell	214.2	40	708	36	19.7	5-36
A. K. Giles	148	17	610	28	21.8	4-27
R. B. Tranter	126.1	25	495	22	22.5	5-16
K. Robinson	114	23	358	15	23.9	6-36
P. Fitzgerald	44	2	231	9	25.7	2-17
D. M. Pursglove	92	5	396	14	26.4	2-5
D. Robeson	58.2	0	311	10	31.1	3-14

Also bowled: D. J. Smith 1-0-1-1; C. Nixon 19-3-62-7; P. R. Corner 3-0-13-1; G. R. Crampton 3-0-14-1; G. E. Dalton 13-1-46-3; D. Edwards 15-0-68-3; Grayson 3-0-27-1; Thomas 4-2-28-1; M. Petrie (guest) 11-1-70-2; M. J. Sewell 2-0-25-0.
Leading Catchers: R. J. Loader 19; D. Robeson 13; J. R. Knowlson 10.
Regular Wicket Keepers: R. J. Loader, D. Robeson, J. R. Knowlson.

Matches 1976

24 April H	Caversham 207-7 dec. Giles 3-35	RUASCC 196-4 Sewell 60, Loader 28 Ansell 25	Drawn
28 April A	RUASCC 199-4 dec. Dalton 52, Sewell 32 Knowlson 49 Loader 31	Owls 99	Won by 100 runs
2 May A	RUASCC 195-6 dec. Sewell 35, Ansell 32 Crampton 42* Knowlson 28*	Students' 3rd XI 132-9 Knowlson 3-18 Giles 3-31	Drawn
5 May A	RUASCC 127-4 dec. Ansell 27 Pearce 21	Royal Ascot 130-4 Ansell 3-6	Lost by 6 wickets
6 May A	Wokingham Schoolmasters 83 Tranter 5-34 Robeson 3-14	RUASCC 70 D. Smith 17	Lost by 13 runs (limited overs)
9 May A	Students' 2nd XI 176-6 dec.	RUASCC 144-6 Giles 58* Knowlson 35	Drawn
12 May A	RUASCC 211-6 dec. Loader 67, Sewell 53 Tranter 41	Wokingham 213-6 Petherick 3-31	Lost by 4 wickets
19 May H	RUASCC 149-6 Butler 45 Pearce 41*	Employees 107 Knowlson 5-47	Won by 42 runs (limited overs)
22 May H	Green Park 164 Ansell 5-36 Petherick 3-33	RUASCC 165-2 Thomas 70 Loader 56	Won by 8 wickets
23 May A	RUASCC 98 Loader 40	Christ Church College 99-2	Lost by 8 wickets

26 May	A	L. S. E. Staff 139-8 dec. Petherick 4-44	RUASCC 141-5 Ansell 32, Loader 30 Knowlson 30	Won by 5 wickets
27 May	A	RUASCC 117 Tranter 47	Reading All Stars 120-3	Lost by 3 runs (overs match)
30 May	H	Surrey University Staff 130 Robinson 4-35 Ansell 3-17	RUASCC 122 Sewell 52, Loader 22 Naysmith 7-57	Lost by 8 runs
2 June	A	RUASCC 81-6 dec. Loader 35 Sewell 24*	Bramshill Police College 83-6 Ansell 3-26	Lost by 4 wickets
5 June	A	RUASCC 115 Knowlson 41, Giles 31	Woodley 116-4	Lost by 6 wickets
8 June	A	Reading Bluecoat School 186-6 dec. Petherick 2-18	RUASCC 190-5 Sewell 86* Hay 24	Won by 5 wickets
9 June	A	RUASCC 161 Loader 30, Giles 24	Reading School All Stars 162-1	Lost by 9 wickets
12 June	H	RUASCC 232-7 Ansell 102, Sewell 52 Pearce 32*	Allen & Unwin 197-8 Stretfield 132* Knowlson 4-73	Drawn
13 June	A	RUASCC 156-8 dec. Sewell 73 Robeson 22*	Leckford 159-3 Budd 74	Lost by 7 wickets
23 June	A	RUASCC 105 Yates 9-32, Ansell 31 Petherick 26* Pearce 23	Students' 1st XI 106-5 Giles 3-40	Lost by 5 wickets
24 June	A	Abingdon 163-5 dec.	RUASCC 108-9 Sewell 25 Bannister 22	Drawn
26 June	H	RUASCC 153 Ansell 69 Pearce 31	Reading Lawyers 115-9 Nixon 7-33	Drawn

30 June	A	Shiplake College 169-3 dec. Ansell 4-38	RUASCC 159-4 Sewell 68*	Drawn
3 July	A	Checkendon 101 Robinson 6-36 Ansell 3-24	RUASCC 102-6 Dobbs 31* Hoskins 25	Won by 4 wickets
7 July	H	Reading Lawyers 196-4 dec.	RUASCC 197-4 Ansell 71*, Sewell 46 Hay 29	Won by 6 wickets
11 July	H	Mandarins 166 Giles 3-24 Ansell 3-27	RUASCC 119-3 Ansell 45 Sewell 39*	Won by 7 wickets

Sir George Edwards Trophy: Semi-Final (limited overs)

14 July	H	L. S. E. 176-8 Petherick 3-14 Robinson 2-36	RUASCC 177-5 Knowlson 78* Butler 28	Won by 5 wickets

Sir George Edwards Trophy: Final (limited overs)

15 July	H	Surrey University Staff 237-8 Petherick 4-36 Giles 2-67	RUASCC 201 Butler 57 Knowlson 38 Ansell 34, Giles 24*	Lost by 36 runs
21 July	H	Bramshill Police College 102 Giles 4-27 Knowlson 3-24	RUASCC 106-4 D. Smith 40 Redfern 31	Won by 6 wickets
28 July	H	Royal Ascot 216-7 dec. Giddings 3-24	RUASCC 117 Crampton 18	Lost by 99 runs
1 Aug.	H	Green Park 151-8 Petherick 6-28	RUASCC 111-9 D. Smith 40 Knowlson 30	Drawn
5 Aug.	H	RUASCC 124-4 Crampton 47 Knowlson 34	Employees 90-8 Petherick 3-24 Giddings 3-15	Won by 34 runs (22 overs match)
11 Aug.	H	RUASCC 100-8 dec. Tranter 34 Crampton 28	S. M. S. Hermitage 90 Petherick 4-37 Tranter 3-24	Won by 10 runs

14 Aug.	H	RUASCC 157 Loader 38 Petherick 30 Robeson 27	Mandarins 96-7 Petherick 3-30	Drawn
15 Aug.	A	RUASCC 84 Jempson 6-25 Petherick 19 Wright 18	West Ilsley 85-2	Lost by 8 wickets
21 Aug.	A	Mapledurham 218-3 Johnson 100*	RUASCC 140 Ansell 79 Petherick 27*	Lost by 78 runs
22 Aug.	A	Stoke Row 178-1 dec. Searby 86* Clark 50*	RUASCC 150-5 D. Smith 61 Petherick 38*	Drawn
29 Aug.	A	Caversham 41 Tranter 5-16 Petherick 3-24	RUASCC 45-5 Tranter 19*	Won by 5 wickets
5 Sept.	H	Hurst 120 Petherick 5-28 Tranter 3-27	RUASCC 87 Knowlson 20	Lost by 33 runs

1977

Captain: J. R. Knowlson
Vice Captain: A. K. Giles
Fixture Secretary: M. J. Sewell
Team Secretaries: G. R. Crampton
D. M. Pursglove
Treasurer: R. D. Pearce

Played 34 Won 13 Lost 9 Drawn 12

Jim Knowlson's second year as skipper. It began with a match at Hurst on April 24th when snow fell and hot soup was served!

Outstanding newcomer to the scene was Alan Rugman ('home' for one year from Canada) whose remarkable consistency with the bat brought him 586 runs for an average of 39. But it was Mike Sewell who again topped the averages with over 750 runs for the second consecutive season, including 97 not out against the Mandarins. Mike Butler rejoined the Club to play some fine innings and Jim Knowlson and Roger Loader also had good seasons with the bat. Tranter and Giles, batting in the lower middle order often added runs. Peter Crane, George Norman and Australian newcomer Joe Gartner became valuable members of the Club — all three, at times, making important contributions on the field.

Richard Tranter and Dave Petherick bowled 469 overs between them, but it was George Norman, amongst the more regular bowlers, who topped the averages. Leg spinners (Pursglove and Fitzgerald) began to be entrusted with more work and collected a couple of dozen wickets each for an identical average of 14 runs. One measure of the depth of the batting was that Peter Fitzgerald had to wait until August 21st to face his first ball — only to be bowled by it!

New fixtures were played against University College London, Exeter University Staff (in the Sir George Edwards Trophy) and the N. I. R. D., whilst fixtures were happily renewed against Reading Police and Newbury, last played in 1966 and 1970 respectively. Defeat was avoided at Christ Church College for the first time (but victory was beyond us) and another typically low scoring game at Royal Ascot was won when Norman and Giles pegged the home side to 114, chasing 134. The third draw was recorded in the last four encounters with the Students' 1st XI. In the first round of the Sir George Edwards Trophy (at Southampton) 214 for 8 against Southampton was not good enough, but the next day 228 for 5 left Exeter with the wooden spoon.

It was a happy season with the record number of wins of the previous season (13) being equalled from four fewer games played — the result of a wet summer. An outstanding feature of the Club's cricket was the really very high standard of fielding that was frequently displayed — not exactly a traditional feature of staff sides. Skipper Jim Knowlson paid special tribute to this at the A. G. M. and mentioned in particular the ground fielding of David Petherick, Dai Edwards, George Norman, Peter Crane, Mike Butler, David Bannister and Alan Rugman and the catching of Joe Gartner, Bob Pearce, Roger Loader, David Smith and Graham Crampton. He was, of course, unlikely to mention the fact that during his two years of captaincy the side was handled by a cricketer who always knew what was going on and, much more often than not, knew how to respond to it.

At the A. G. M., also, Keith Robinson's name was added to the very short list of Honorary Life Members in recognition of his

110

high class bowling for so many years. He had begun bowling for the Club in its earliest days — back in the middle 1950s — and didn't retire until the end of the 1976 season.

Batting 1977

	Matches	Innings	N. O.	Runs	H. Score	Av.
M. J. Sewell	22	22	7	751	97*	50.1
A. R. Rugman	21	20	5	586	64	39.1
J. R. Knowlson	20	16	4	318	63	26.5
M. D. S. Butler	14	13	0	335	64	25.8
D. J. Ansell	24	21	4	383	73*	22.5
R. B. Tranter	25	17	4	273	63	21.0
A. K. Giles	15	11	3	167	64	20.9
R. J. Loader	26	25	3	438	55	19.9
A. Fisher	10	9	0	157	42	17.4
D. Bannister	6	6	0	102	35	17.0
D. Edwards	8	5	2	45	27*	15.0
D. J. Smith	6	5	1	55	30*	13.7
G. Norman	20	13	4	110	27	12.2
G. R. Crampton	17	14	5	109	44	12.1
D. Robeson	10	7	1	66	51*	11.0
W. D. Redfern	7	5	0	53	32	10.6
P. R. Crane	10	8	2	61	33	10.2
J. A. Gartner	17	11	2	74	29	8.2
D. J. Petherick	26	9	4	36	14*	7.2
R. D. Pearce	18	14	3	79	21	7.2
D. M. Pursglove	19	5	3	9	4*	4.5

Also batted: P. J. Giddings 0*, 17, 20; D. Russell 20, 13, 19, 2; C. Browne 12*; P. Fitzgerald 0; W. J. Straker-Nesbit 0.

Bowling 1977

	Overs	Mdns	Runs	Wkts	Av.	Best
R. Smith	23	5	64	6	10.7	5-35
G. Norman	163.1	24	535	38	14.1	5-11
P. Fitzgerald	79	10	342	24	14.2	5-31
D. M. Pursglove	103	10	387	27	14.3	5-47
J. R. Knowlson	21.5	2	91	6	15.2	2-3
R. B. Tranter	237	51	736	39	18.9	7-44
D. J. Petherick	232.2	47	709	35	20.3	5-41
A. K. Giles	87	8	340	16	21.2	4-28
J. A. Gartner	70	5	305	14	21.8	5-42
D. J. Ansell	72.2	4	265	12	22.1	3-33
A. R. Rugman	94.5	9	351	12	29.3	2-5
P. J. Giddings	31	4	114	3	38.0	2-41
P. R. Crane	28	3	137	1	137.0	1-24

Also bowled: C. Browne 9-3-22-1; M. Petrie 13-2-43-1; M. D. S. Butler 4-0-29-0.
Leading Catchers: R. J. Loader 9; R. B. Tranter 8.
Regular Wicket Keepers: R. J. Loader and D. Robeson

Matches 1977

24 April	A	Hurst 133-9 dec. Petherick 5-41 Tranter 3-17	RUASCC 120-9 Rugman 35	Drawn
27 April	A	Students' 3rd XI 125 Petherick 3-11 Norman 3-21 Pursglove 3-28	RUASCC 126-3 Bannister 35 Fisher 31 Edwards 27	Won by 7 wickets
30 April	H	Caversham 153 Norman 5-59	RUASCC 129 Tranter 63	Lost by 24 runs
7 May	A	RUASCC 123 Sewell 50	Students' 2nd XI 108-7	Drawn
11 May	A	RUASCC 124-4 dec. Rugman 37* Knowlson 35 Bannister 25	Bramshill Police College 125-6 Fitzgerald 3-22	Lost by 4 wickets
15 May	A	RUASCC 149-8 dec. Butler 50 Sewell 44 Rugman 30	Christ Church College 145-8 Ansell 3-33 Petherick 3-40	Drawn
18 May	A	Wokingham 200-7 dec.	RUASCC 133	Lost by 67 runs
21 May	H	Green Park 75 Pursglove 4-31	RUASCC 76-4 D. J. Smith 30*	Won by 6 wickets
24 May	A	Bluecoat School 93 Fitzgerald 4-21	RUASCC 96-5 Rugman 29 Loader 26	Won by 5 wickets
26 May	A	RUASCC 194-1 dec. Sewell 86* Rugman 42* Loader 37	Shiplake College Wanderers 195-5	Lost by 5 wickets
28 May	H	RUASCC 198-8 dec. Rugman 50* Sewell 41, Gartner 29	Reading Lawyers 200-4	Lost by 6 wickets

1 June	A	RUASCC 134	Royal Ascot 114	Won by
		Fisher 28	Norman 5-32	20 runs
			Giles 4-28	
5 June	A	RUASCC 161-5 dec.	Surrey University	Won by
		Rugman 60	Staff 77	84 runs
		Sewell 29	Fitzgerald 5-31	
		Knowlson 25		
8 June	H	U. C. L. 111-6 dec.	RUASCC 113-2	Won by
			Sewell 47	8 wickets
			Loader 27*	
22 June	A	Students' 1st XI	RUASCC 114-5	Drawn
		214-4 dec.	Rugman 30	
25 June	H	Allen & Unwin 149	RUASCC 150-1	Won by
		Tranter 5-45	Sewell 66*	9 wickets
		Petherick 3-19	Knowlson 63	
28 June	H	Wokingham	RUASCC 114-4	Won by
		Schoolmasters 113-5	Loader 38, Butler 29	6 wickets
			Norman 27	(limited overs)
3 July	A	RUASCC 78	Checkendon 79-9	Lost by
			Norman 5-11	1 wicket
			Petherick 4-23	
6 July	H	Bramshill Police	RUASCC 119-6	Drawn
		College 163-7 dec.	Knowlson 39	
			Loader 27*	

Sir George Edwards Trophy: First Round (limited overs)

12 July	A	RUASCC 214-8	Southampton 215-5	Lost by
		Butler 59	Tranter 3-46	5 wickets
		Knowlson 44		
		Ansell 27		

Sir George Edwards Trophy: Losers Tie (limited overs)

13 July	A	RUASCC 228-5	Exeter 185-2	Won by
		Rugman 64	Hitchcock 84*	43 runs
		Sewell 49, Ansell 44*		
17 July	H	Mandarins 187-7 dec.	RUASCC 178-5	Drawn
			Ansell 73*	
			Loader 34, Crane 33	

20 July	H	Royal Ascot 156-6 dec. Norman 3-45	RUASCC 154-8 Loader 55	Drawn
23 July	H	Employees 110 Pursglove 5-47	RUASCC 111-3 Robeson 51* Knowlson 44*	Won by 7 wickets
27 July	H	RUASCC 189-6 dec. Loader 55 Crampton 44 Rugman 39*	Reading Lawyers 140-7 Fitzgerald 3-50	Drawn
31 July	A	Caversham 96 Norman 5-17 Tranter 3-30	RUASCC 60 Giles 33	Lost by 36 runs
10 Aug.	H	Reading Police 163-7 dec.	RUASCC 164-3 Ansell 50, Sewell 43* Fisher 42	Won by 7 wickets
13 Aug.	H	RUASCC 175-6 dec. Sewell 97* Rugman 34	Mandarins 176-3	Lost by 7 wickets
21 Aug.	H	Stoke Row 86 Pursglove 4-22	RUASCC 88-9 Tranter 31	Won by 1 wicket
27 Aug.	H	Mapledurham 159-7 dec. R. Smith 5-35	RUASCC 87-7	Drawn
28 Aug.	H	Checkendon 162-4 dec. Ansell 3-50	RUASCC 162-4 Sewell 70* Ansell 64	Won by 6 wickets
4 Sept.	H	RUASCC 172-7 dec. Giles 64, Tranter 31* Ansell 31	Hurst 117-6 Pursglove 4-21	Drawn
11 Sept.	A	RUASCC 207-6 dec. Butler 55, Tranter 38 Redfern 32	N. I. R. D. 125-9 Tranter 7-44	Drawn
21 Sept.	A	Newbury 168 Gartner 5-42 Petherick 3-44	RUASCC 77-5 Bannister 26	Drawn

1978

Captain: M. J. Sewell
Vice Captain: A. K. Giles
Fixture Secretary: M. D. S. Butler
Team Secretaries: G. R. Crampton
                            D. M. Pursglove
Treasurer: R. B. Tranter

Played 42　Won 18　Lost 11　Drawn 12　Tied 1

This was in various ways the most extraordinary season in the history of the Club. Mike Sewell began his four-year spell as captain and much of what happened reflected credit on him. With Mike Butler as his new fixture secretary no fewer than 48 fixtures were arranged, including six new opponents, three of which remain, Leighton Park School (who gave us a real scare), Whitchurch and Reading. In the event, rain reduced the matches played to 42 — still three more than in any previous year — 18 of which were won — a new record. In total, three-quarters of all matches played were won, drawn or tied.

Mike Pursglove and Graham Crampton (in their second year as joint team secretaries) worked hard in consultation with Sewell, to field strong teams, especially in the key matches, and Richard Tranter completed a strong committee as Treasurer — taking over from Bob Pearce who had done the job assiduously for seven years.

Using his resources with great thought, not least his slow bowlers (Fitzgerald, Pursglove and Giles took 64 wickets between them),

117

Sewell invited sides to seek victory and they were often defeated. With his own 765 runs, nearly 600 from Butler, over 400 from Knowlson and over 300 each from five other batsmen (Ansell, Gartner, Loader, Tranter and Crane) Sewell often had runs to play with. In one remarkable week in May, Sewell, Butler and Knowlson all made centuries. There were also some remarkable feats with the ball: the Australian newcomer Roger Smith captured 9 Lawyers' wickets for 28 producing an unlikely victory after RUASCC had scored only 72; Alan Robiette, who had often failed to get the success he deserved, was unplayable on a humid day at S. M. S. Hermitage and took 8 for 29, whilst Peter Fitzgerald, Dave Petherick and George Newman all enjoyed hauls of 7 wickets in a match. Petherick and Tranter again provided the spearhead of the attack.

In addition to Roger Smith (who was to be available for one season only) valuable newcomers included postgraduate Steve Adkins, John Benton and Andy Baum in his first season proper.

There were now too many games for all the outstanding ones to be mentioned in this brief commentary but the 'double' over our friendly rivals, the Reading Lawyers, was especially enjoyed, as was an eight-wicket victory over Bluecoat School, chasing 174; a clear cut victory over the formidable Surrey University Staff side; and victories against long-standing and doughty opponents like Leckford, S. M. S. Hermitage and Newbury. Would that Wokingham could have been added to the list!

Mike Sewell, however, brought the team to its peak in the Sir George Edwards Trophy played at Surrey. Set to get 197 in the first round by King's College London, some hard hitting by Petherick and Tranter, when all seemed lost, took the side into the final in which (for a change) Southampton were never let off the hook — dismissed for 105 and an eight-wicket victory took the Trophy away from Surrey who had held it for its first three years. The RUASCC performance in that final was as high as could be expected from cricket at this level. Not least, the fielding had been an important feature of the Club's cricket all

118

the season, with Peter Crane outstanding, taking no less than 26 catches. Richard Tranter was not far behind with 19.

What a season! The whole committee was re-elected — and we waited expectantly for 1979.

Batting 1978

	Matches	Innings	N. O.	Runs	H. Score	Av.
C. H. Walker	5	5	2	132	56*	44.0
M. J. Sewell	26	25	7	765	113*	42.5
M. D. S. Butler	21	21	5	569	117*	35.6
J. R. Knowlson	20	17	2	427	111*	28.5
D. J. Ansell	17	15	0	351	66	23.5
J. A. Gartner	25	20	4	358	44	22.4
R. J. Loader	18	17	2	334	82	22.3
R. B. Tranter	35	27	7	335	45	16.7
R. Smith	19	11	6	82	20*	16.4
P. R. Crane	32	26	7	309	57*	16.3
A. K. Giles	27	23	5	281	39	15.6
A. E. Baum	9	6	0	83	46	13.8
G. R. Crampton	19	18	1	229	36	13.3
D. Robeson	10	10	1	114	38*	12.7
S. W. Adkins	13	12	0	149	65	12.4
D. J. Petherick	31	15	2	152	31	11.6
W. D. Redfern	12	11	1	84	40	8.4
G. Norman	9	5	1	32	22	8.0
R. D. Pearce	18	15	2	94	17	7.2
D. Edwards	13	12	0	72	25	6.0
D. M. Pursglove	27	12	6	31	10*	5.1
A. G. Robiette	13	7	1	12	6	2.0
P. Fitzgerald	18	7	2	7	4	1.4

Also batted: D. Smith 69*, 0; J. Benton 51*, 7; J. A. Giles 36, 1;
D. G. Hay 4, 16, 9; S. Hussain 17, 0; B. Curtis 7, 2, 2;
N. Bather 11*.

Bowling 1978

	Overs	Mdns	Runs	Wkts	Av.	Best
G. Norman	72	17	172	20	8.6	7-29
N. Bather	20	1	74	7	10.6	4-39
A. G. Robiette	67	9	232	19	12.2	8-29
D. J. Petherick	299.5	68	896	63	14.2	7-62
R. Smith	154	21	530	37	14.3	9-28
R. B. Tranter	275	45	909	63	14.4	5-13
D. M. Pursglove	137.2	26	503	33	15.2	6-32
P. , Fitzgerald	88	6	412	24	17.2	7-29
P. R. Crane	108	20	313	18	17.4	3-8
A. K. Giles	148.2	18	522	28	18.6	5-32
J. A. Gartner	160	18	627	18	36.9	3-10

Also bowled: M. D. S. Butler 6-0-26-1; S. W. Adkins 8-1-56-0;
D. J. Ansell 11-1-77-0; J. Benton 4-1-15-0; D. Edwards 1-0-4-0.
Leading Catchers: P. R. Crane 26; R. B. Tranter 19; M. D. S. Butler 11;
Regular Wicket Keepers: D. J. Ansell and D. Robeson

Matches 1978

23 April	H	Hurst 119 (mistakenly scored as 129)	RUASCC 131-7 Sewell 44	Won by 3 wickets
28 April	H	RUASCC 152-6 dec. Ansell 47 Gartner 37*	Caversham 120-7 Tranter 3-14	Drawn
10 May	H	Students' 3rd XI 167-9 dec. Tranter 5-33	RUASCC 109-6 Ansell 56	Drawn
17 May	A	Wokingham 162-4 dec. R. Smith 4-28	RUASCC 86 Edwards 25 Gartner 21	Lost by 76 runs
20 May	H	RUASCC 247-3 dec. Knowlson 111* Redfern 40 Loader 39, Butler 33*	Green Park 48 Fitzgerald 7-29	Won by 199 runs
21 May	A	N. I. R. D. 113 Tranter 3-13	RUASCC 116-5 Sewell 52*	Won by 5 wickets
23 May	A	Bluecoat School 174-5 dec. Woolhead 120	RUASCC 175-2 Butler 117*	Won by 8 wickets
25 May	A	RUASCC 201-5 dec. Sewell 113* Tranter 33* Loader 28	Shiplake College Wanderers 174-9 Tranter 4-39	Drawn
27 May	H	RUASCC 181 Ansell 66 Sewell 23, Norman 22	Reading Lawyers 149 Tranter 5-13 Norman 3-33	Won by 32 runs
31 May	A	RUASCC 117 Giles 39, Crampton 29	Royal Ascot 118-9 Norman 7-29	Lost by 1 wicket
4 June	A	RUASCC 195-3 dec. Loader 82 Sewell 61 R. Smith 20*	Surrey University Staff 114 Tranter 4-16 Fitzgerald 3-35	Won by 81 runs

Date		Opponent	RUASCC	Result
7 June	A	Reading School All Stars 127-4 Pursglove 3-13		Abandoned as a draw
11 June	H	Southampton University Academic Staff 193-7 dec. Robiette 3-44 Gartner 3-58	RUASCC 156-6 Knowlson 76 Giles 37	Drawn
14 June	H	U. C. L. Staff 161-4 dec.	RUASCC 160-9 Knowlson 59 Crampton 36	Drawn
18 June	A	Leckford 68 Norman 3-8 Gartner 3-10	RUASCC 71-0 Butler 42* Crampton 23*	Won by 10 wickets
21 June	H	Students' 1st XI 193-5 dec. Soza 85*, Smith 3-56	RUASCC 122 Knowlson 25 Tranter 23, Butler 20	Lost by 71 runs
24 June	A	Leighton Park School 130 Tranter 4-19 Pursglove 3-19	RUASCC 132-7 Crane 33 Giles 24*	Won by 3 wickets
27 June	H	Wokingham Schoolmasters 107 Petherick 6-56 Tranter 3-26	RUASCC 111-3 Sewell 61* Knowlson 21	Won by 7 wickets
1 July	H	RUASCC 172 Loader 39 Butler 29, Sewell 30 Crampton 27	Students' 2nd XI 139-9 Petherick 4-28 Gartner 3-24	Drawn
2 July	A	Checkendon 121 Robiette 3-22 Tranter 3-10	RUASCC 100 Sewell 27 Butler 21	Lost by 21 runs
5 July	A	RUASCC 138 Loader 59 Tranter 45	Bramshill Police College 141-9 Petherick 5-70 Tranter 3-53	Lost by 1 wicket
9 July	H	Sonning 186-7 dec. Giles 3-40	RUASCC 88 Knowlson 27	Lost by 98 runs

Sir George Edwards Trophy: First Round (limited overs)

12 July	A	KCL Staff 197	RUASCC 200-9	Won by
		Risby 110	Sewell 38	1 wicket
		Crane 3-19	Petherick 31	
			Knowlson 27	
			Tranter 28*	

Sir George Edwards Trophy: Final (limited overs)

13 July	A	Southampton	RUASCC 108-2	Won by
		University Staff 105	Sewell 51*	8 wickets
		Smith 3-25	Knowlson 25	
			Butler 22*	
16 July	H	Mandarins 132	RUASCC 135-2	Won by
		Pursglove 6-32	Walker 56*	8 wickets
			Loader 38*, Crane 26	
19 July	H	Royal Ascot 205	RUASCC 146-5	Drawn
		O'Shaughnessy 88*	Crane 57*	
		Petherick 6-57	Robeson 38	
		R. Smith 4-51		
22 July	H	RUASCC 162-6 dec.	Employees 163-5	Lost by
		D. Smith 60*		5 wickets
		Gartner 31		
23 July	A	Caversham 136-8 dec.	RUASCC 111-9	Lost by
		Bather 4-39	J. Giles 36	25 runs
		Giles 3-40	Robeson 32	(limited overs)
26 July	H	RUASCC 72	Reading Lawyers 65	Won by
		Giles 16	R. Smith 9-28	7 runs
29 July	H	Wokingham 172-9 dec.	RUASCC 154-7	Drawn
		R. Smith 4-17	Loader 33	
			Crampton 32	
			Gartner 21*	
5 Aug.	A	RUASCC 82	Fairmile Hospital 83-1	Lost by
		Gartner 36	Makepeace 56*	9 wickets
12 Aug.	H	Mandarins 176-8 dec.	RUASCC 141-8	Drawn
		Tranter 5-61	Gartner 44, Crane 32	

124

13 Aug. H	West Ilsley 129	RUASCC 132-4	Won by
	Burrows 74*	Sewell 53*	6 wickets
	Bather 3-35	Giles 29*	
	Crane 3-8	Butler 28	
19 Aug. H	Stoke Row 152-8 dec.	RUASCC 152	Tied
		Butler 49, Sewell 45	
27 Aug. H	Checkendon 201-9 dec.	RUASCC 139-6	Drawn
	Giles 5-32	Sewell 64*	
	Petherick 4-77	Ansell 25	
30 Aug. H	Whitchurch 160	RUASCC 161-5	Won by
	Petherick 7-62	Ansell 58	5 wickets
	Smith 3-30	Benton 51*	
3 Sept. H	RUASCC 233	Reading 170-9	Drawn
	Butler 73	Fitzgerald 4-48	
	Adkins 65, Tranter 42	Pursglove 3-9	
9 Sept. H	RUASCC 89	Hurst 90-4	Lost by
	Ansell 17	Petherick 3-20	6 wickets
10 Sept. A	RUASCC 184	N. I. R. D. 102	Won by
	Walker 54	Pursglove 3-11	82 runs
	Tranter 34	Crane 3-14	
	Adkins 31, Baum 31	Giles 3-29	
13 Sept. A	S. M. S. Hermitage 46	RUASCC 50-3	Won by
	Robiette 8-29	Gartner 30*	7 wickets
17 Sept. H	RUASCC 123	Mapledurham 125-4	Lost by
	Crane 41, Gartner 20	Tranter 3-28	6 wickets
20 Sept. A	RUASCC 148	Newbury 121	Won by
	Baum 46	Pursglove 3-35	27 runs

1979

Captain: M. J. Sewell
Vice Captain and Treasurer: R. B. Tranter
Fixture Secretary: M. D. S. Butler
Team Secretaries: G. R. Crampton
                     D. M. Pursglove

Played 47 Won 13 Lost 22 Drawn 12

Mike Sewell enjoyed his second year as captain and again gave
immense effort to the job. Mike Butler had arranged
54 matches — which early season rain reduced to 47 — and
Mike Pursglove and Graham Crampton laboured yet again to
put teams into the field. No fewer than ten new fixtures were
included against Nettlebed, Shinfield, Wellington Schoolmasters,
Littlewick Green, Savernake Forest, Tilehurst, the
Gloucestershire Clergy, Hartley Wintney, Warborough and
Knowl Hill.

For some unaccountable reason — with almost the same pool of
players as in the previous season — defeats rose from 11 to 22.
Only three victories were recorded in the first 21 games leading
up to the Sir George Edwards Trophy — and it was perhaps a
truer reflection of the available talent that the Trophy was
retained with resounding victories against the Southampton and
Surrey Staff sides. Both victories were based on very good
outcricket and controlled batting — except perhaps, for George
Norman's frantic 38 against Surrey! — and it was a special
pleasure for Mike Sewell to receive the Trophy from the hands
of our longstanding friend and opponent from Shiplake

126

College — J. D. Eggar — late of Oxford University, Hampshire and Derbyshire and now retiring from his headmastership.

From then on the tide turned, with 10 victories from the remaining 26 games. But at the end of the season, it had been memorable for isolated and individual performances rather than for the sustained match winning cricket of the previous year. Outstanding individual performances were Mike Sewell's new record number of appearances in a season (38) and his 1,170 runs (the first Club player to exceed 1,000 in a season). Close behind him came Mike Butler with three centuries and Dave Petherick's record number of overs bowled (355) and wickets taken (66). Richard Tranter and Mike Pursglove were also heavily bowled. Tony Giles edged himself to the top of the bowling averages but perhaps the best slow bowling feat of the season was Joe Gartner's 5 for 57, on a good wicket, out of Abingdon's 173 for 7.

The outstanding newcomer to the Club was undoubtedly Martin Avis — late of Reading C. C. After a half century on his first outing he had a lean time until his class showed itself with 46 not out and 78 in the two Trophy games. Eventually he averaged nearly 30, bowled nearly 100 overs and displayed a throw from the covers likely to put any wicket keeper on his back! Perhaps the lack of one regular and consistent wicket keeper had something to do with the disappointing results. Another newcomer, postgraduate Neill Morrison also added to the Club's fielding strength, bowled well and often looked capable of making more runs than he did.

Apart from the two Trophy matches, there were other memorable matches including the dismissal (by Petherick and Pursglove) of Savernake Forest for a mere 91 after RUASCC had struggled to 108; a 3 wicket win in a low scoring match against the Gloucestershire Clergy; and the 186 for 0 put on by Butler and Sewell in answer to Warborough's 184 for 3. It was also pleasing to push both our keen rivals Royal Ascot and Caversham very close to defeat, Peter Crane and Mike Butler both scoring 101 not out against Caversham. And we were not averse to a 9 wicket victory over Wokingham — albeit not their Wednesday side.

But it was not all glory. Two defeats in a season were inflicted on us (for only the second time in our history) by the Students' 2nd XI and (for the first time) by other keen rivals, the Reading Lawyers. There was a first defeat also from N. I. R. D. Perhaps the season was all summed up one Sunday afternoon late in September, when playing Knowl Hill, on an 'unusual' wicket, in constant rain and terrible light, our opponents batted until tea time for 47 all out and RUASCC chalked up its thirteenth win of the season — by one wicket! Nobody blamed the committee, they were all re-elected for 1980 and Mike Sewell became the first holder of the new Club Award for 'an outstanding contribution to the season'. His 1,170 runs allied to the keenness of his captaincy would not easily be surpassed.

Batting 1979

	Matches	Innings	N. O.	Runs	H. Score	Av.
M. D. S. Butler	20	19	3	740	114*	46.2
M. J. Sewell	38	38	10	1,170	101*	41.8
M. R. Avis	18	18	3	431	78	28.7
G. Norman	12	7	3	110	38	27.5
J. R. Knowlson	22	22	4	469	58*	26.1
P. R. Crane	27	25	5	340	101*	17.0
J. A. Gartner	20	17	2	241	65*	16.1
A. E. Baum	18	16	3	207	38*	15.9
R. B. Tranter	33	24	4	297	39	14.8
A. K. Giles	16	11	1	143	50	14.3
S. W. Adkins	16	15	2	183	45	14.1
J. Benton	13	11	0	141	42	12.8
D. J. Ansell	14	12	1	131	34	11.9
R. J. Loader	27	26	1	283	41	11.5
G. R. Crampton	28	26	0	294	50	11.3
R. D. Pearce	20	11	0	103	44	9.3
J. P. Wieczorek	9	6	1	46	26*	9.2
N. A. D. Morrison	17	13	3	77	11	7.7
W. D. Redfern	8	7	1	44	18	7.3
M. Owen	19	15	2	89	28	6.8
P. Fitzgerald	23	9	4	30	9	6.0
D. J. Petherick	35	23	5	99	18	5.5
D. M. Pursglove	33	23	12	53	11	4.8
M. I. Mackness	9	8	0	30	14	3.7
A. R. Jones	11	6	3	11	5*	3.7

Also batted: M. D. Biddiss 17; Bryglin 15; A. Hay 8; M. Petrie 4*, 4, 0, 4*;
C. Ritson 0*, 0; C. H. Walker 0.

Bowling 1979

	Overs	Mdns	Runs	Wkts	Av.	Best
A. K. Giles	82.3	10	308	21	14.7	3-24
D. J. Petherick	355	77	1,058	66	16.0	5-22
M. R. Avis	92.3	8	357	22	16.2	4-29
R. B. Tranter	272.3	43	948	51	18.6	4-4
P. Fitzgerald	121.1	8	575	30	19.2	5-44
D. M. Pursglove	173.5	10	734	37	19.8	5-52
P. R. Crane	93.5	15	324	16	20.2	2-8
J. A. Gartner	124.3	14	500	22	22.7	5-42
N. A. D. Morrison	133.5	22	457	16	28.6	5-61
G. Norman	54	11	178	6	29.7	3-39
A. R. Jones	60	11	216	5	43.2	1-9

Also bowled: S. W. Adkins 1-0-2-0; D. J. Ansell 2-0-11-1; J. Benton 4-0-30-2; M. D. Biddiss 12-0-56-1; M. Petrie 11-1-47-2.
Leading Catchers: A. E. Baum 14; P. R. Crane 12; J. A. Gartner 11.
Regular Wicket Keepers; A. E. Baum, R. J. Loader, J. R. Knowlson and D. J. Ansell.

Matches 1979

22 April	H	RUASCC 156 Sewell 52	Hurst 26-2	Abandoned as a draw
28 April	H	Caversham 161-8 dec. Petherick 5-29	RUASCC 110 Butler 37, Sewell 26	Lost by 51 runs
6 May	A	Nettlebed 103 Tranter 3-39	RUASCC 89 Butler 32	Lost by 14 runs
9 May	H	U. C. L. 154 Petherick 5-54 Pursglove 3-16	RUASCC 155-3 Avis 57* Knowlson 35 Ansell 28*	Won by 7 wickets
12 May	A	N. I. R. D. 60-9 Fitzgerald 4-11	RUASCC 61-7 (24.1 overs) Sewell 24*	Won by 3 wickets (limited overs)
22 May	A	Bluecoat School 150-4 dec. Fitzgerald 3-44	RUASCC 104-4 Sewell 56*	Drawn
30 May	H	RUASCC 131 Tranter 39, Crane 27	Royal Ascot 4-0	Abandoned as a draw
6 June	H	Bramshill Police College 136 Pursglove 4-24 Petherick 3-51	RUASCC 120-8 Knowlson 45 Sewell 32	Drawn
9 June	A	Shinfield 126 Petherick 5-25 Tranter 3-34	RUASCC 119-6 Ansell 34	Drawn
10 June	H	RUASCC 151-8 dec. Sewell 71*, Avis 41	Students' 2nd XI 152-4	Lost by 6 wickets
14 June	A	Wellington Schoolmasters 80-5	RUASCC 67-6 Butler 34 Sewell 21*	Lost by 13 runs (limited overs)
16 June	H	RUASCC 153 Sewell 39 Butler 28, Steel 7-31	Students' 1st XI 157-5 Soza 83	Lost by 5 wickets
17 June	A	RUASCC 152-9 dec. Butler 41, Owen 28 Tranter 25*	Leckford 153-6 Tranter 3-40	Lost by 4 wickets

131

20 June	A	RUASCC 162 Sewell 53, Baum 29 Tranter 25	Reading School All Stars 163-2	Lost by 8 wickets
23 June	H	RUASCC 202-2 dec. Sewell 101* Gartner 49*	Leighton Park School 191 Petherick 4-44	Won by 11 runs
26 June	H	RUASCC 139 Crampton 34 Sewell 29	Wokingham Schoolmasters 142-6 Petherick 3-57	Lost by 4 wickets
28 June	A	Abingdon 173-7 dec. Gartner 5-57	RUASCC 98	Lost by 75 runs
30 June	H	RUASCC 127-9 dec. Baum 35*	Students' 2nd XI 128-3	Lost by 7 wickets
1 July	A	Checkendon 162-5	RUASCC 129-7 Butler 86	Drawn
4 July	H	Littlewick Green 176-3 dec.	RUASCC 110 Sewell 46 Gartner 26	Lost by 66 runs
7 July	H	RUASCC 197-4 dec. Butler 100* Sewell 55*	Employees 165-9 Giles 3-24 Tranter 3-29 Avis 2-20, Cheetham 97*	Drawn

Sir George Edwards Trophy: First Round (limited overs)

11 July	H	Southampton University Academic Staff 130 (38.5 overs) Avis 4-29	RUASCC 131-1 Sewell 61* Avis 46*	Won by 9 wickets

Sir George Edwards Trophy: Final (limited overs)

12 July	H	RUASCC 229-8 (40 overs) Avis 78, Norman 38 Butler 30, Ansell 28	Surrey University Staff 122 Petherick 2-12 Giles 2-15, Gartner 2-21 Tranter 2-23	Won by 107 runs
15 July	H	Mandarins 178 Pursglove 5-52	RUASCC 181-3 Knowlson 58* Crampton 47 Loader 41	Won by 7 wickets

132

18 July	A	RUASCC 198-9 dec. Giles 50 Crane 39*, Loader 27	Royal Ascot 87-6 Petherick 3-20		Drawn
22 July	A	RUASCC 216-1 dec. Crane 101* Butler 101*	Caversham 151-7 Norman 3-39		Drawn
25 July	H	Whitchurch 141 Gartner 5-42 Tranter 3-32	RUASCC 142-5 Sewell 65* Knowlson 49		Won by 5 wickets
28 July	A	RUASCC 108 Avis 63	Savernake Forest 91 Petherick 5-33 Pursglove 4-19		Won by 17 runs
29 July	H	Wokingham 102 Tranter 5-27 Giles 3-33	RUASCC 103-1 Knowlson 42* Adkins 30*		Won by 9 wickets
1 Aug.	H	Reading Lawyers 113 Pursglove 3-35	RUASCC 83		Lost by 30 runs
2 Aug.	A	Staff College Owls 130-9 dec.	RUASCC 128-9 Knowlson 36 Crane 31		Lost by 2 runs (limited overs)
5 Aug.	A	RUASCC 149-8 dec. Gartner 65*	Tilehurst 83 Fitzgerald 4-34 Tranter 3-8		Won by 66 runs
8 Aug.	H	RUASCC 177-6 dec. Crampton 50 Loader 27*	Reading Police 180-6 Tranter 4-47		Lost by 4 wickets
11 Aug.	H	RUASCC 118 Pearce 44	Mandarins 122-2		Lost by 8 wickets
12 Aug.	A	RUASCC 117 Knowlson 34 Norman 28*	West Ilsley 120-4		Lost by 6 wickets
15 Aug.	H	RUASCC 139 Sewell 35	N. I. R. D. 143-8 Morrison 5-61		Lost by 2 wickets
18 Aug.	H	RUASCC 167-8 dec. Butler 55 Benton 42	Nettlebed 170-6		Lost by 4 wickets

22 Aug.	A	Whitchurch 166-9 dec. Fitzgerald 5-60	RUASCC 114-5 Avis 36*	Drawn
26 Aug.	H	RUASCC 185-8 dec. Sewell 65, Avis 56 Knowlson 30*	Checkendon 134-4	Drawn
29 Aug.	A	Gloucestershire Clergy 111 Tranter 4-19 Fitzgerald 3-46	RUASCC 112-7 Baum 38* Loader 35	Won by 3 wickets
2 Sept.	H	Reading 186 Petherick 3-22 Tranter 3-41, Dyer 88	RUASCC 75-2 Butler 43	Drawn
5 Sept.	A	RUASCC 59	Hartley Wintney 61-5 Petherick 5-22	Lost by 5 wickets
8 Sept.	H	Warborough 184-3 dec.	RUASCC 186-0 Butler 114* Sewell 58*	Won by 10 wickets
12 Sept.	A	S. M. S. Hermitage 147-9 dec. Morrison 3-37	RUASCC 94 Tranter 29	Lost by 53 runs
16 Sept.	A	Mapledurham 148-8 dec. Fitzgerald 5-44	RUASCC 100 Wieczorek 26* Nolan 7-49	Lost by 48 runs
23 Sept.	A	Knowl Hill 47 Tranter 4-4 Petherick 4-24	RUASCC 48-9 Giles 23	Won by 1 wicket
29 Sept.	H	RUASCC 193-9 Sewell 49 Adkins 45	Reading Lawyers 194-1 Messenger 91* Frost 75*	Lost by 9 wickets

134

1980

Captain: M. J. Sewell
Vice Captain and Treasurer: R. B. Tranter
Team Secretaries: G. R. Crampton
                       D. M. Pursglove
Fixture Secretary: M. D. S. Butler

Played 52 Won 20 Lost 9 Drawn 23

After a chilly start on 20th April, the Club registered a string
of victories during the warmth of May and did not meet with
convincing defeat until well into June. By then Mike Sewell
had had the misfortune to break his arm and did not play
again until mid August. However, despite the loss of his runs,
a rotating captaincy and a depressingly wet summer, the Club
prospered, playing more than 50 matches for the first time in
its history, recording a record number of wins (20) and avoiding
defeat in no less than 83% of its matches: another record.

Apart from the continuing interest that Mike Sewell took in
the side while his arm was recovering, a major reason for success
was the large intake of new players (especially postgraduates)
providing a total pool of 35 regular players. Amongst the
newcomers Renny Ison added style to the early batting, whilst,
in their different ways, John Elder, Tony Seraphin, Andy Orme,
Trevor Ridley and Peter Hotten, all bowled well and helped to
compensate for the loss of David Petherick — an outstanding
opening bowler of recent seasons who moved to Checkendon
and played only three times for the Club in 1980. Other valuable
newcomers included Ivan Thomson, Steve Fleming, Garry

Whitelam and Kerry Patterson — whilst Mike Biddiss had his first full season with the Club and, like many of the others, showed all-round capabilities.

New fixtures were played against Farley Hill, Finchampstead, Coley Park and Braywick. Amongst many satisfying games, victories over our Students' 2nd XI and Shiplake College Wanderers, chasing over 200 on both occasions and a rare 7-wicket win over Newbury will stand out in memory. With the bat Martin Avis, Mike Butler and David Ansell all recorded not-out centuries. Martin Avis topped the averages (66.7), Mike Butler scored most runs (769) and Mike Sewell, despite missing three months of the season, scored a remarkable 667 runs for an average of 55.6. There were three century partnerships — the best of which was no doubt the opening stand of 154 by 'Jim and the Professor' in a drawn game against the Students' 1st XI. Outstanding amongst the bowlers was Mike Pursglove's 50 wickets (and his 1 run, scored, he still remembers, on 10 September at Farley Hill) and David Petherick's 8 for 20 against University College, London. Over the season it was remarkable that, despite a large battery of 'seam' bowlers, the 'slow' bowlers (of various pedigree) collected 131 wickets: 38% of the total. Richard Tranter was again a tireless all-rounder.

In Exeter, in July, the Club relinquished its two-year hold on the Sir George Edwards Trophy to the Exeter University Staff who beat Southampton in the final. RUASCC avoided the wooden spoon, beating Surrey in the losers play-off. At the end of the season Mike Butler was given the Club Award in recognition of his runs and his remarkable job, over three years, as Fixture Secretary. Mike Sewell was re-elected for his fourth season as Captain, equalling the record previously held by David Ansell.

Two Vice Captains (D. M. Pursglove and R. B. Tranter) were appointed to help with the increasing administrative load associated with over 50 fixtures.

Graham Crampton relinquished his job as Team Secretary after a long and efficient stint, and the Club bade farewell to Steve Adkins and the genial and talented Australian, Joe Gartner.

Reading University Academic Staff
Cricket Club

SOCIAL

in the Pavillion
on Thursday 6 July at 8 to 11 pm

presentation of Single Wicket Trophy

7s 6d single   Dancing   15s double

Playing members are asked to provide a plate of savoury food

Ticket for the social, 1967

Batting 1980

	Matches	Innings	N. O.	Runs	H. Score	Av.
M. R. Avis	13	12	5	467	112*	66.7
M. J. Sewell	21	19	7	667	89*	55.6
M. D. S. Butler	25	23	2	769	104*	38.4
R. B. Tranter	24	15	8	229	73*	32.7
R. W. Ison	21	19	1	526	69	29.2
J. R. Knowlson	17	16	3	351	72	27.0
D. J. Ansell	23	22	3	510	103*	26.8
J. A. Gartner	17	14	0	324	70	23.1
G. R. Crampton	16	15	2	292	66*	22.5
J. S. Elder	13	10	3	157	55*	22.4
A. J. Benton	25	20	5	311	45	21.7
R. J. Loader	18	18	1	368	78	21.6
G. Norman	12	12	1	233	57	21.2
S. W. Adkins	10	9	0	188	59	20.9
A. Seraphin	13	12	4	159	37	19.9
P. R. Crane	9	8	0	156	40	19.5
A. Orme	14	4	2	36	25*	18.0
P. M. Hotten	16	13	3	155	29	15.5
A. K. Giles	13	11	4	105	34	15.0
I. Thomson	10	8	0	112	34	14.0
S. Fleming	15	8	2	82	34	13.7
W. D. Redfern	13	11	2	121	34	13.4
M. Owen	12	11	2	101	34	11.2
M. D. Biddiss	17	9	4	56	29*	11.2
R. D. Pearce	14	9	1	61	22*	7.6
M. I. Mackness	7	4	0	30	16	7.5
N. A. D. Morrison	7	5	0	32	15	6.4
G. E. Whitelam	15	13	0	69	18	5.3
J. P. Wieczorek	9	6	2	21	11*	5.2
D. Edwards	6	5	0	25	16	5.0
P. Fitzgerald	21	10	3	23	8 -	3.3
T. Ridley	18	7	2	13	7	2.6
A. G. Robiette	14	6	3	7	4*	2.3
D. M. Pursglove	28	6	2	1	1	0.2

Bowling 1980

	Overs	Mdns	Runs	Wkts	Av.	Best
D. J. Petherick	35.3	7	113	12	9.4	8-20
I. Thomson	26	3	102	10	10.2	4-17
P. M. Hotten	23.5	2	110	9	12.2	3-4
M. R. Avis	83	20	259	18	14.4	5-41
J. A. Gartner	108	13	383	26	14.7	7-35
P. Fitzgerald	114	15	578	35	16.5	4-32
D. M. Pursglove	199.3	19	868	50	17.6	8-31
R. B. Tranter	235.5	47	790	43	18.4	4-24
T. Ridley	113	31	367	19	19.3	4-17
G. E. Whitelam	34	3	158	8	19.7	2-15
M. Hatton	25	1	84	4	21.2	2-31
A. Orme	122.3	28	584	27	21.6	6-21
P. R. Crane	32.4	7	114	15	23.8	3-31
P. Oakley	15.5	1	73	3	24.3	2-39
K. Patterson	57	12	177	7	25.3	3-15
J. S. Elder	76.1	11	341	13	26.2	5-47
N. A. D. Morrison	71.3	10	291	10	29.1	4-42
A. Seraphin	108.3	18	328	10	32.8	2-19
S. Fleming	61.4	7	264	7	37.7	2-8
A. G. Robiette	77.2	20	303	5	60.6	2-37
A. K. Giles	70.2	5	354	5	70.8	2-28
M. Petrie	43	6	153	2	76.5	2-28

Also bowled: A. J. Benton 4-1-29-3; C. Jones 13-0-59-2;
A. Amin 6-1-23-1; G. Norman 4-2-6-0; D. J. Ansell 1-0-10-0.
Leading catchers: G. E. Whitelam 10; D. J. Ansell, A. J. Benton 9;
J. R. Knowlson, M. J. Sewell 8.
Regular wicket keepers: 7 members of the Club shared this task, the
most frequent of whom was D. J. Ansell.

Batting 1980 continued
Also batted: A. E. Baum 7, 28, 51; D. J. Petherick 24, 0, 3; M. Hatton 0,
4, 0*; K. Patterson 0, 0, 0*; M. Petrie 3*, 2*; P. Oakley 1*, 1;
A. Amin 9; D. Donkin 6; D. Smith 1*.

Matches 1980

20 April	H	RUASCC 191-8 dec. Gartner 70, Crane 40 Knowlson 24	Hurst 195-9 Gartner 5-67 Tranter 3-62	Lost by 1 wicket
26 April	H	Caversham 226-7 dec. Fitzgerald 4-54	RUASCC 202-9 Gartner 44, Crane 29 Sewell 29, Benton 27	Drawn
27 April	H	Students' 2nd XI 200-9 dec. Pursglove 5-48	RUASCC 202-4 Sewell 73, Avis 65* Loader 46	Won by 6 wickets
30 April	A	RUASCC 116 Norman 31	Royal Ascot 67 Tranter 3-22	Won by 49 runs
4 May	H	Students' 1st XI 223-4 dec. Patel 103*	RUASCC 187-2 Sewell 89 Knowlson 72	Drawn
6 May	H	RUASCC 92 Petherick 24	U. C. L. 64 Petherick 8-20	Won by 28 runs
10 May	A	N. I. R. D. 91-6 (25 overs)	RUASCC 92-3 (24 overs) Benton 26	Won by 7 wickets
11 May	A	Woodley 189-4 dec.	RUASCC 166-7 Butler 36, Redfern 34 Ansell 33	Drawn
14 May	A	Gloucestershire Clergy 81	RUASCC 85-6 Ansell 25, Gartner 20	Won by 4 wickets
18 May	H	Students' 3rd XI 140 Pursglove 8-31	RUASCC 141-4 Loader 50, Butler 40*	Won by 6 wickets
22 May	A	Shiplake College Wanderers 218-7 dec. Partridge 104	RUASCC 219-7 Ison 69, Ansell 63* Loader 37	Won by 3 wickets
24 May	H	RUASCC 138 Butler 69, Loader 33 Gartner 20	Mandarins 128 Avis 4-51 Tranter 3-36	Won by 10 runs
25 May	A	RUASCC 163-6 dec. Butler 75, Ansell 32	Leckford 139-8 Fitzgerald 4-61	Drawn

28 May	H	RUASCC 129-4 Tranter 73* Gartner 31	Reading Police	Abandoned as a draw
1 June	A	RUASCC 237-3 dec. Avis 112*, Ison 64 Norman 57	Surrey University Staff 153 Orme 6-21	Won by 84 runs
4 June	A	RUASCC 151-4 dec. Avis 63, Hotten 29 Seraphin 22	Bramshill Police College 141-7 Avis 5-41	Drawn
7 June	A	RUASCC 99 Fleming 34	Stoke Row 101-4	Lost by 6 wickets
8 June	H	RUASCC 201-8 dec. Loader 78, Butler 53	Southampton University Academic Staff 205-3 Fahy 100	Lost by 7 wickets
12 June	H	RUASCC 201-3 dec. Crampton 66, Butler 63, Ison 30 Ansell 22	Bluecoat School 160 Ridley 4-17, Hotten 3-11	Won by 41 runs
15 June	H	Tilehurst 154-5 dec.	RUASCC 137-8 Benton 45 Knowlson 42	Drawn
18 June	A	Reading School All Stars 163-9 dec.	RUASCC 134-8 Crampton 32, Avis 29 Elder 26	Drawn
21 June	A	RUASCC 131 Gartner 30 Seraphin 28	Leighton Park School 134-4	Lost by 6 wickets
26 June	A	Wellington Schoolmasters 115 Tranter 4-24	RUASCC 113-8 Tranter 23, Ison 20	Lost by 2 runs (24 overs)
28 June	A	Nettlebed 141-8 dec.	RUASCC 113-5 Avis 41*, Thomson 34	Drawn
29 June	A	RUASCC 168-6 dec. Ison 67, Gartner 27 Thomson 26 Orme 25*	Warborough 91 Patterson 3-15 Orme 3-18	Won by 77 runs

141

6 July	A	RUASCC 82-7 dec.	Checkendon 83-1	Lost by 9 wickets
12 July	H	RUASCC 186-6 dec. Butler 50, Ison 50 Baum 28	Mandarins 125-8 Fitzgerald 3-26	Drawn

Sir George Edwards Trophy: First Round (limited overs)

16 July	A	Southampton University Academic Staff 178-8	RUASCC 123 Knowlson 57 Ansell 46	Lost by 55 runs

Sir George Edwards Trophy: Losers' Tie (limited overs)

17 July	A	RUASCC 157-9 Ison 43, Butler 31 Giles 25	Surrey University Staff 123	Won by 34 runs
23 July	H	Whitchurch 135-7 dec. Thorley 99 Avis 4-21	RUASCC 136-4 Adkins 35, Ansell 32 Sewell 24*	Won by 6 wickets
27 July	A	Hurst 167-7 dec. Orme 4-26	RUASCC 130-8 Norman 57, Butler 21	Drawn
30 July	H	RUASCC 206-5 dec. Avis 55, Baum 51 Crane 24	Reading Lawyers 190-5 Pursglove 5-25	Drawn
2 Aug.	H	RUASCC 132 Crane 33, Ison 27	Staff College Owls 93 Orme 4-10	Won by 39 runs
3 Aug.	H	RUASCC 212-4 dec. Ison 67*, Adkins 59 Butler 48, Pearce 22*	Knowle Hill 125 Pursglove 4-31 Tranter 3-17	Won by 87 runs
6 Aug.	H	Reading Police 214-4 dec.	RUASCC 117-7 Biddiss 29*, Ansell 27	Drawn
14 Aug.	A	Abingdon 207-2 dec.	RUASCC 92-3	Abandoned as a draw
16 Aug.	H	RUASCC 181-4 dec. Butler 104*, Sewell 46	Nettlebed 125-7	Drawn
20 Aug.	H	Royal Ascot 230-5 dec. Blake 127	RUASCC 135-8 Loader 34, Giles 34 Sewell 24	Drawn
24 Aug.	H	RUASCC 196-9 dec. Butler 65, Seraphin 37 Owen 34, Ison 21	Checkendon 156-8 Morrison 4-42	Drawn

27 Aug.	A	Whitchurch 183-9 dec.	RUASCC 143-4	Drawn
		Thomson 3-46	Sewell 57*	
			Knowlson 45, Avis 23*	
31 Aug.	H	Reading 176-6 dec.	RUASCC 177-5	Won by
			Sewell 60, Adkins 45	5 wickets
3 Sept.	H	Stoke Row 188-6 dec.	RUASCC 112-5	Drawn
		Morrison 4-63	Benton 36*	
			Knowlson 21	
6 Sept.	H	Coley Park 146	RUASCC 152-0	Won by
		Pursglove 5-41	Ansell 103*	10 wickets
		Benton 3-6	Hotten 27*	
7 Sept.	A	Knowl Hill 189-9 dec.	RUASCC 142-8	Drawn
		Thomson 4-17	Sewell 64*	
		Tranter 4-64	Norman 20	
10 Sept.	A	RUASCC 123	Farley Hill 126-3	Lost by
		Crampton 49		7 wickets
		Knowlson 31		
		Sewell 25		
16 Sept.	H	R. U. Employees 116	RUASCC 118-2	Won by
		Gartner 7-35	Elder 55*, Benton 37*	8 wickets
		Tranter 3-42	Hotten 21	
17 Sept.	A	Newbury 123	RUASCC 125-3	Won by
		Hotten 3-24	Crampton 57*	7 wickets
		Pursglove 3-24	Redfern 26*	
20 Sept.	H	Mapledurham 196-5 dec.	RUASCC 141-6	Drawn
			Sewell 64*	
21 Sept.	H	Braywick 149-9	RUASCC 150-5	Won by
		Tranter 4-32	Benton 42*,	5 wickets
			Gartner 41, Tranter 25*	
24 Sept.	H	N. I. R. D. 132	RUASCC 126-9	Drawn
		Fitzgerald 4-32	Adkins 33, Sewell 31*	
		Biddiss 3-13	Norman 24	
27 Sept.	H	Reading Lawyers 72-0	RUASCC	Abandoned as a draw
28 Sept.	H	Finchampstead 199-5	RUASCC 56	Lost by 143 runs

1981

Captain: M. J. Sewell
Vice Captain and Treasurer: R. B. Tranter
Vice Captain and Team Secretary: D. M. Pursglove
Fixture Secretary: D. J. Ansell
Team Secretary: A. J. Benton

Played 46 Won 11 Tied 1 Lost 10 Drawn 24

The weather at the start of this season was so cold and wet that not much cricket was really enjoyed until well into June. No fewer than 7 successive matches were cancelled in May.

Mike Sewell again skippered the side with his own particular brand of determination and only 10 out of 46 games were lost. For the second time in his career Sewell completed 1000 runs, although headed in the averages by Ivan Thomson (42.7), Mike Butler (41.5), and Tony Giles (40.2, in a late flourish) and Martin Avis (39.9). Peter Fitzgerald was the leading wicket taker (40) and John Elder had the best average amongst the more heavily used bowlers with 39 wickets for 13.8 runs each. Mike Pursglove had a hat trick against Eversley. Richard Tranter bowled more overs than anyone else (206) and with a similar batting and bowling average (around 22) he was again the Club's leading all-rounder.

In a welcome 'guest' appearance, Graham Dalton — who left the Club early in 1976 and had done nothing more energetic since then than shepherding — took 5 for 37 against Caversham. Alan Rugman was another welcome and successful guest, back briefly from Canada. Such reappearances are always welcomed

144

by the Club, and Peter Crane, John Benton and Ivan Thomson, who left the Club at the end of the season, were reminded of this.

The Club started well in the Sir George Edwards Trophy recording its highest ever score in any match, 259 for 7 (in a mere 40 overs), to beat Exeter — only to 'blow' the final by 8 runs against Southampton. Amongst the more satisfying matches of the season was a last ball victory in a low scoring match against Bramshill Police College (91 for 9 in reply to 90), a 9-wicket win in reply to 175 for 9 by the Mandarins, a rare 6-wicket victory against Checkendon, another last-ball victory against long-standing rivals, Newbury, and in the last match a convincing win by 4 wickets over N. I. R. D., having once been 25 for 5 chasing 121.

At the end of the season in which two new fixtures were played — Merry Mowers and Eversley — Mike Sewell's efforts as captain and batsman, not only in 1981 but over four successive seasons, were acknowledged when he became the first player to receive the Club Award for a second time.

Batting 1981

	Matches	Innings	N. O.	Runs	H. Score	Av.
I. Thomson	15	13	4	384	63	42.7
M. D. S. Butler	21	21	3	747	89*	41.5
A. K. Giles	10	9	4	201	69*	40.2
M. R. Avis	13	12	3	359	84	39.9
M. J. Sewell	36	36	4	1010	80	31.6
J. R. Knowlson	19	19	3	397	63*	24.8
R. B. Tranter	23	19	4	332	58	22.1
R. W. Ison	17	15	0	283	64	18.9
D. J. Ansell	16	15	1	200	36	14.3
A. G. Robiette	12	6	5	14	6*	14.0
A. J. Benton	30	28	4	323	13	13.5
J. S. Elder	18	15	5	139	31*	12.6
A. Seraphin	18	14	1	129	19	9.9
P. R. Crane	6	6	0	59	26	9.8
D. Edwards	6	4	0	34	19	8.5
P. M. Hotten	19	16	3	106	22	8.1
M. I. Mackness	7	4	1	24	14	8.0
M. D. Biddiss	23	16	3	103	25	7.9
D. M. Pursglove	31	10	6	30	8	7.5
T. Ridley	22	11	5	42	9	7.0
R. D. Pearce	19	17	3	92	24	6.6
J. P. Wieczorek	15	14	1	72	33	5.5
M. Owen	13	9	1	46	18	5.3
G. Lee	6	1	0	4	4	4.0
P. Fitzgerald	30	13	7	23	6*	3.8
W. D. Redfern	8	8	1	25	9	3.6
C. Miles	6	5	1	12	9*	3.0
P. Oakley	6	6	3	9	5*	3.0

Also batted: G. R. Crampton 55, 0, 12; T. Walden 1, 22, 11*;
D. Williams 0, 2, 6*; S. Banyard 15*, 5; A. E. Baum 36, 12;
A. E. Orme 0, 0*; A. R. Rugman 45, 25; J. Short 0, 9; M. Wheeler 17, 0;
R. Cooper 1; G. E. Dalton 6; Dodds 7; J. A. Gartner 4*;
N. A. D. Morrison 0; D. J. Petherick 1; D. Smith 0; C. H. Walker 12;
M. Petrie, N. Stockton 0*.

146

Bowling 1981

	Overs	Mdns	Runs	Wkts	Av.	Best
G. Lee	43	9	139	11	12.6	5-19
J. S. Elder	172	31	538	39	13.8	5-31
A. G. Robiette	80	13	265	19	13.9	6-27
A. Orme	32	11	72	5	14.4	2-14
N. Stockton	12	0	44	3	14.7	3-19
A. Seraphin	150	35	441	24	18.4	4-4
P. Fitzgerald	171	11	808	40	20.2	5-27
M. R. Avis	112	21	365	18	20.3	3-15
P. Oakley	29	7	103	5	20.6	2-1
P. M. Hotten	54	12	190	9	21.1	2-10
R. B. Tranter	206	36	728	34	21.4	5-22
I. Thomson	35	3	132	6	22.0	2-34
P. R. Crane	31	1	118	5	23.6	4-26
A. K. Giles	30	5	153	6	25.5	2-29
M. D. Biddiss	163	32	527	19	27.7	4-49
T. Ridley	165	36	618	19	32.5	4-47
D. M. Pursglove	164	13	722	21	34.4	4-69
A. R. Rugman	20	6	75	2	37.5	1-32
D. Edwards	12	0	90	2	45.0	1-23
M. Wheeler	15	1	57	1	57.0	1-18
N. A. D. Morrison	13	3	62	0	∞	0-26

Also bowled: J. A. Gartner 9-0-26-3; D. Williams 7-0-46-1;
M. I. Mackness 5-0-31-0; M. D. S. Butler 1-0-5-0;
G. R. Crampton 1-0-9-0; G. E. Dalton 12-2-37-5;
D. J. Petherick 15-5-36-4.
Leading catchers: D. J. Ansell 14; J. R. Knowlson 12; R. W. Ison 11;
R. B. Tranter 10; M. J. Sewell 9.
Regular wicket keepers: D. J. Ansell & J. R. Knowlson

Matches 1981

19 April H	Hurst 128	RUASCC 131-5	Won by
	Tranter 5-22	Sewell 64, Butler 53	5 wickets
	Gartner 3-26		
25 April H	Caversham 192-6 dec.	RUASCC 91-4	Drawn
		Benton 27*, Ansell 22	
29 April A	RUASCC 117-7 dec.	Royal Ascot 77-6	Drawn
	Avis 63, Elder 29	Avis 3-18	
2 May H	Newbury 131-9 dec.	RUASCC 110-8	Drawn
	Seraphin 4-4	Tranter 23	
6 May A	U. C. L. 114-8 dec.	RUASCC 83-6	Drawn
		Elder 32*	
9 May A	N. I. R. D. 68-8	RUASCC 68-9	Tie
		Tranter 35	(limited overs)
13 May A	Farley Hill 122	RUASCC 85-8	Drawn
	Robiette 6-27	Avis 43*	
4 June A	RUASCC 124-5	Merry Mowers 125-3	Lost
	Baum 36, Butler 34		(limited overs)
6 June A	RUASCC 150	Stoke Row 112-6	Drawn
	Thomson 55		
	Tranter 43		
7 June A	Southampton	RUASCC 26-0	Abandoned
	University Academic		as a draw
	161-6 dec.		
10 June H	Students' 1st XI	RUASCC 118	Lost
	170-9 dec.	Ison 40, Butler 33	
	Crane 4-26	Crane 26	
14 June H	Tilehurst 142-7 dec.	RUASCC 124-7	Drawn
		Sewell 55*, Pearce 24	
		Knowlson 23	
17 June A	Reading School	RUASCC 232-8	Drawn
	All Stars 247-4 dec.	Crampton 55	
	Dindar 119*	Benton 43	
	Seraphin 3-59	Avis 56	

20 June	H	Leighton Park School 164 Avis 3-15	RUASCC 155-6 Thomson 63	Drawn	
23 June	H	Wokingham Schoolmasters 143-3	RUASCC 144-5 Butler 81	Won (limited overs)	
25 June	A	Wellington Schoolmasters 127-5 Seraphin 3-29	RUASCC 56-8	Lost (limited overs)	
27 June	A	Nettlebed 132-8 dec. Fitzgerald 5-27	RUASCC 96-8 Avis 50	Drawn	
28 June	A	RUASCC 227-3 dec. Butler 89, Sewell 80 Knowlson 47	Staff College Owls 106 Fitzgerald 5-51 Elder 3-33	Won	
1 July	H	Littlewick Green 160 Ridley 4-47	RUASCC 100-7 Knowlson 34 Benton 23*, Hotten 21	Drawn	
4 July	H	Shinfield 143-8 dec. Tranter 5-43	RUASCC 92-6 Tranter 51*	Drawn	
5 July	A	RUASCC 107 Benton 37, Ison 21	Checkendon 111-1	Lost by 9 wickets	
8 July	A	Bramshill Police College 90 Elder 5-36	RUASCC 91-9 Elder 21*	Won by 1 wicket	
12 July	H	Mandarins 175-9 dec. Fitzgerald 3-18 Avis 3-53	RUASCC 176-1 Butler 70* Knowlson 63* Sewell 37	Won by 9 wickets	

Sir George Edwards Trophy: First Round (limited overs)

15 July	A	RUASCC 259-7 Butler 85, Sewell 53 Thomson 44*	Exeter University Erratics 166	Won by 93 runs	

Sir George Edwards Trophy: Final (limited overs)

16 July	A	Southampton University Academic Staff 172 Petherick 3-15	RUASCC 164 Avis 52, Sewell 25 Thomson 22	Lost by 8 runs	

19 July	A	Hurst 220-4 dec. Fitzgerald 2-35	RUASCC 135 Ison 25, Biddiss 25 Benton 20	Lost by 85 runs
25 July	A	Braywick 153-8 dec. Fitzgerald 4-39	RUASCC 126-7 Thomson 50 Hotten 22	Drawn
26 July	A	Caversham 161-9 dec. Dalton 5-37	RUASCC 154-8 Ison 64, Sewell 33	Drawn
29 July	H	Reading Lawyers 169-6 dec. Biddiss 4-47	RUASCC 171-9 Thomson 53* Ansell 36, Sewell 32	Won by 1 wicket
2 Aug.	H	Knowl Hill 159-6 dec. Tranter 4-46	RUASCC 86-8 Ansell 34	Drawn
9 Aug.	H	Leckford 238-5 dec. Tranter 3-59	RUASCC 138-8 Tranter 58, Butler 35 Ansell 35	Drawn
13 Aug.	A	Abingdon 179-6 dec. Stockton 3-19	RUASCC 138-8 Butler 54 Wieczoreck 33	Drawn
15 Aug.	H	RUASCC 178-5 dec. Sewell 55 Knowlson 39 Thomson 32	Nettlebed 149-9 Lee 5-19	Drawn
19 Aug.	H	Royal Ascot 172-4 dec.	RUASCC 135-9 Rugman 45 Knowlson 38	Drawn
23 Aug.	H	Checkendon 131 Elder 7-37	RUASCC 132-4 Sewell 48, Butler 27 Rugman 25	Won by 6 wickets
26 Aug.	A	Whitchurch 234-9 dec.	RUASCC 128-4 Sewell 45, Ison 42	Drawn
30 Aug.	A	Reading A XI 122-9 dec. Elder 5-31	RUASCC 119 Sewell 31, Ison 23	Lost by 3 runs
2 Sept.	H	Stoke Row 161-7 dec. Avis 3-23	RUASCC 127-9 Sewell 57, Crane 22	Drawn

150

5 Sept.	H	RUASCC 157-5 dec. Sewell 65, Benton 42 Walden 22	Woodley 159-6 Lee 3-45	Lost by 4 wickets
6 Sept.	H	RUASCC 185-9 dec. Sewell 63, Butler 26 Giles 23*	Eversley 185-8 Pursglove 4-69	Drawn
9 Sept.	H	Farley Hill 204-4 dec.	RUASCC 158-7 Knowlson 40 Sewell 31, Avis 23	Drawn
12 Sept.	H	RUASCC 144-8 dec. Giles 57* Thomson 27	Warborough 145-1	Lost by 9 wickets
16 Sept.	A	Newbury 139-7 dec. Fitzgerald 3-24 Tranter 3-50	RUASCC 140-6 Butler 47, Sewell 38	Won by 4 wickets
19 Sept.	A	Mapledurham 158-7 dec. Ridley 3-44	RUASCC 8-0	Abandoned as a draw
20 Sept.	H	Braywick 114-9 dec.	RUASCC 115-2 Butler 62, Sewell 37	Won by 8 wickets
23 Sept.	H	N. I. R. D. 121-9 dec. Fitzgerald 3-20 Elder 3-29	RUASCC 122-6 Giles 69*	Won by 4 wickets

1982

Captain and Fixture Secretary: D. J. Ansell
Vice Captain and Treasurer: R. B. Tranter
Vice Captain and Team Secretary: D. M. Pursglove
Team Secretary: T. Ridley

Played 50 Won 15 Lost 15 Drawn 20

With David Ansell back as Captain, after a break of six years, the Club 'broke even' in a season that will probably be remembered more for a number of unusual incidents and matches than for the overall quality of the cricket played. As usual, an inability to field strong sides regularly led to uneven performances — high-lighted by a 10-wicket win and a 7-wicket defeat in successive matches in May — whilst the failure to have either a regular opening pair of batsmen or bowlers contributed to a lack of good starts.

With injury restricting Mike Butler to only 13 innings and Jim Knowlson to a mere 7, it was as well that Mike Sewell had yet another prolific summer with the bat scoring 1,439 runs for an average of 45. Mike Butler (two centuries and an average of 46.1), newcomer John Budd (621), Martin Avis (438), David Ansell (417) and Renny Ison (336) all made decisive contributions with the bat at times, but no-one came within half of Mike Sewell's aggregate — nor could equal his 1 for 1 with the ball! Andy Orme headed the bowling averages with 38 wickets for 16.1 runs apiece and might have returned better figures but for an inexplicable (but, happily shortlived) loss of control in mid -season. Mike Pursglove took most wickets (48) but, no doubt disappointed himself in being

152

unable to extend a rich early harvest into the rest of the season. Peter Fitzgerald, recovered from serious injury to his hand, collected 37 wickets and was a popular winner of the Club Award. Nobody, amongst the bowlers however, worked harder — or more unluckily — than Trevor Ridley. As usual, Richard Tranter's all-round effort was invaluable, well supported in that role by Mike Biddiss and Peter Hotten.

Amongst the more extraordinary events of the season was the early season 10-wicket victory over Newbury, who had declared with 228 on the board. Butler and Sewell scored these runs in a mere 90 minutes, recording the highest score for any wicket in the Club's history, and Mike Butler's 156 not out (his second successive century) was the highest-ever individual score. The 10-wicket victory was repeated against out old adversaries at Shiplake, three weeks later, and nothing was more exciting than Richard Tranter putting the last ball of the home match against Leckford comfortably into Elmhurst Road to overtake their 195 for 6. Even more unusual was the 4 scored by Trevor Ridley off the last ball (all run, including an overthrow!) to beat Wokingham by three wickets. Checkendon (with 122 not out from Doug Powell) must have felt reasonably safe with 231 for 4 on the board only to lose by 6 wickets (Avis 86 not out), while John Budd's 96 not out (after the Club was 39 for 5 chasing 180 for 3) led to a 3-wicket victory over Eversley and has been described by those who have seen many of them as one of the very best innings played in the Club's history. A glance at the match scores will show that there were many other performances which were less glorious, and few who were involved will forget the ferocity with which Print of Tilehurst (160) and Dindar of Reading School All Stars (117) set about our attack.

A comfortable victory, at home, in the first round of the Sir George Edwards Trophy, against Exeter, promised well, but the final was one of the few games rained off in 1982, and, for the first time, the Trophy was not awarded. In total, the

Club managed to play 50 matches and, not surprisingly with such a full fixture list, there were, for the first time in our history, no new opponents. All in all, it was a happy season and there was no happier and (for those who played with him) nostalgic sight than that of Graham Dalton, visiting as an external examiner from Aberdeen, walking out to bat against the Reading School All Stars and collecting 25 runs with all his old aplomb.

It was not surprising that, at the A. G. M., David Ansell was re-elected Captain (for the sixth time) together with the other principal officers from 1982. When the new season starts, it will be without the help of John Elder, Andy Orme and Peter Hotten all of whom have played hard for the Club in recent seasons, as well as several others, including Mike Hallam and David Crush who played for a season, passing through from East Africa. By the time this book appears, the 1983 nets will probably be over and a fresh season underway — and with it, the second twenty-five years of RUASCC.

Batting 1982

	Matches	Innings	N. O.	Runs	H. Score	Av.
M. D. S. Butler	13	13	4	505	156*	56.1
M. J. Sewell	40	40	8	1439	98*	45.0
A. Amin	9	8	4	152	39	38.0
M. R. Avis	16	16	4	438	86*	36.5
T. Walden	8	8	1	199	60	28.4
R. B. Tranter	27	23	10	369	53*	28.4
J. Budd	27	26	3	621	96*	27.0
R. W. Ison	15	14	0	336	91	24.0
D. J. Ansell	24	21	1	417	87	20.8
G. R. Crampton	12	11	0	198	86	18.0
J. S. Elder	11	10	1	139	61	15.4
M. Roffey	5	5	1	61	30*	15.3
R. D. Pearce	18	16	4	181	35	15.1
J. R. Knowlson	7	7	2	69	22*	13.8
A. Orme	23	17	6	150	29	13.6
M. Hallam	14	12	1	147	32	13.4
A. K. Giles	19	16	1	198	40	13.2
M. D. Biddiss	23	17	3	182	43	13.0
P. M. Hotten	19	19	1	197	59	10.9
P. J. Fitzgerald	23	11	8	32	15*	10.7
P. Berry	10	10	2	79	18	9.9
I. Warburton	21	17	4	119	18	9.1
C. Miles	21	18	0	154	22	8.5
T. Ridley	31	13	8	40	9*	8.0
D. M. Pursglove	32	16	9	26	4*	3.7
J. P. Wieczorek	14	12	0	44	18	3.7
J. Short	9	7	0	22	6	3.3
D. Crush	14	8	1	23	10	3.3
L. Prevost	5	5	0	16	8	3.2
A. G. Robiette	6	5	0	8	3	1.7

Also batted: G. E. Dalton 25; A. Dodd 1; M. Edwards 9;
S. Fleming 15, 31, 0; J. A. Gartner 6; M. Lewis 5, 1, 1; P. Oakley 1;
D. Smith 24; F. Tallett 0; A. Thompson 6*, 1, 0, 2; I. Thomson 4, 39, 0;
C. H. Walker 4, 0.

Bowling 1982

	Overs	Mdns	Runs	Wkts	Av.	Best
A. Orme	202.1	46	611	38	16.1	5-33
J. S. Elder	99.5	21	339	21	16.1	6-24
J. Short	28	10	106	6	17.7	3-27
R. B. Tranter	254.4	43	804	44	18.3	4-28
S. Fleming	21	5	79	4	19.7	3-25
D. M. Pursglove	201	18	954	48	19.9	6-49
M. R. Avis	86.1	18	262	13	20.1	3-22
P. J. Fitzgerald	164.1	4	813	37	21.8	6-89
P. M. Hotten	51.3	6	220	10	22.0	3-33
T. Ridley	323.3	60	1027	43	23.9	6-47
M. D. Biddiss	150	21	635	26	24.4	6-34
A. M. M. Thompson	37	3	149	4	37.2	2-31
D. Crush	71.4	18	226	6	37.7	2-19
M. Hallam	73.1	9	317	8	39.6	4-38
T. Walden	17	0	88	2	44.0	1-28
D. J. Ansell	18	3	89	2	44.5	2-36
I. Warburton	67.5	7	328	7	46.8	2-12
J. Budd	48	1	269	2	134.5	1-31

Also bowled: A. Amin 6-0-39-1; P. Berry 1-0-9-0; J. A. Gartner 4-1-10-1; P. Oakley 10-1-38-0; A. G. Robiette 12-1-37-0; M. J. Sewell 1-0-1-1; I. Thomson 3-0-21-0.
Leading catchers: J. Budd 12; M. D. Biddiss 11; A. K. Giles 9.
Regular wicket keepers: D. J. Ansell & A. K. Giles.

Matches 1982

18 April	H	RUASCC 184-6 dec. Sewell 77*, Butler 38	Hurst 121-8 Tranter 3-15	Drawn
21 April	H	RUASCC 181-7 dec. Biddiss 43, Ansell 36 Pearce 35, Sewell 32	Bramshill Police College 178-7 Hotten 3-33	Drawn
24 April	H	Caversham 177 Ridley 3-38	RUASCC 90 Budd 26	Lost by 87 runs
25 April	H	Students' 2nd XI 154-9 dec. Pursglove 6-49	RUASCC 158-7 Butler 101*	Won by 3 wickets
27 April	A	RUASCC 96 Crampton 26	Royal Ascot 99-8 Pursglove 5-12	Lost by 2 wickets
1 May	H	Newbury 228-9 dec. Fleming 3-25 Tranter 3-56 Pursglove 3-79	RUASCC 232-0 Butler 156* Sewell 60*	Won by 10 wickets
5 May	H	RUASCC 113-6 dec. Sewell 37, Amin 25*	U. C. L. 114-3	Lost by 7 wickets
12 May	A	Farley Hill 199-4 dec. Ridley 3-37	RUASCC 188-9 Ansell 87 Crampton 31, Sewell 20	Drawn
16 May	H	Students' 3rd XI 97 Pursglove 4-12	RUASCC 99-1 Butler 59*, Budd 22*	Won by 9 wickets
18 May	H	RUASCC 114 Avis 58, Hallam 20	Bluecoat School 118-6	Lost by 4 wickets (limited overs)
20 May	A	Shiplake College Wanderers 130-9 dec. Orme 3-22 Ridley 3-37	RUASCC 134-0 Avis 66*, Sewell 52*	Won by 10 wickets
22 May	H	Mandarins 196 Ridley 6-47	RUASCC 151-3 Sewell 64*, Budd 37	Drawn
27 May	H	Merry Mowers 100-6 Tranter 3-16	RUASCC 101-7 Sewell 25	Won by 3 wickets (limited overs)

30 May	A	Leckford 170-5 dec.	RUASCC 157-7 Sewell 51, Tranter 50*	Drawn
5 June	A	Stoke Row 158-6 dec. Orme 3-31	RUASCC 127-9 Hotten 59	Drawn
6 June	H	Southampton University Academic Staff 178-3 dec.	RUASCC 182-9 Butler 61, Sewell 33 Biddiss 22	Won by 1 wicket
9 June	H	Students' 1st XI 239-9 dec. Orme 3-52	RUASCC 152-8 Ansell 37, Giles 24 Avis 22*	Drawn
13 June	H	RUASCC 227-8 dec. Ison 75, Sewell 54 Tranter 30*, Budd 21	Tilehurst 228-2 Print 160	Lost by 8 wickets
16 June	A	RUASCC 223-5 dec. Crampton 86, Avis 64 Dalton 25	Reading School All Stars 224-4 Dindar 117	Lost by 6 wickets
19 June	A	Leighton Park School 119-5 dec. Avis 3-27	RUASCC 123-4 Sewell 42* Thomson 39	Won by 6 wickets
24 June	A	Wellington Schoolmasters 100-7 Short 3-27	RUASCC 88 Sewell 27, Ison 20	Lost by 12 runs (limited overs)
30 June	A	RUASCC 116 Budd 37, Avis 31	Littlewick Green 118-6 Avis 3-22	Lost by 4 wickets
3 July	H	Shinfield 115 Elder 4-42	RUASCC 85-7 Sewell 31	Drawn
4 July	A	RUASCC 107 Sewell 29, Ansell 22	Checkendon 108-1	Lost by 9 wickets
7 July	A	Bramshill Police College 158-4 dec.	RUASCC 100-6 Crampton 22 Pearce 22, Knowlson 22*	Drawn
11 July	H	Mandarins 158 Hallam 4-38	RUASCC 161-8 Budd 83, Hotten 33	Won by 2 wickets
		Sir George Edwards Trophy: First round (limited overs)		
14 July	H	Exeter University Erratics 78-9	RUASCC 80-3 Ansell 28, Avis 27	Won by 7 wickets

Sir George Edwards Trophy: Final

15 July		No play, rain.		
18 July	A	RUASCC 218-6 dec. Ison 91, Tranter 20*	Hurst 196-6 Fitzgerald 6-89	Drawn
21 July	H	Whitchurch 233-2 dec. Thorley 138*	RUASCC 107-6 Sewell 63*, Giles 23	Drawn
24 July	A	Braywick 114 Elder 6-24	RUASCC 107 Tranter 30, Budd 21	Lost by 7 runs
25 July	A	Shinfield 160 Biddiss 6-34	RUASCC 128 Sewell 59	Lost by 32 runs
28 July	H	Reading Lawyers 224-5 dec.	RUASCC 116-9 Giles 32, Budd 29 Sewell 20	Drawn
31 July	H	Knowl Hill 139 Tranter 4-40 Fitzgerald 3-4	RUASCC 131-9 Elder 61	Drawn
7 Aug.	A	Staff College Owls 221-9 dec. Pursglove 3-36 Hotten 3-45	RUASCC 205-6 Sewell 98*, Budd 37 Smith 24	Drawn
8 Aug.	H	Leckford 195-6 dec. Tranter 3-36	RUASCC 200-5 Sewell 88, Budd 44 Orme 29	Won by 5 wickets
12 Aug.	A	Abingdon 175-8 dec. Pursglove 4-50	RUASCC 153-5 Sewell 65*	Drawn
14 Aug.	H	Nettlebed 200-6 dec. Fitzgerald 3-52	RUASCC 137-7 Sewell 58, Ansell 23	Drawn
21 Aug.	H	Wokingham 167 Fitzgerald 4-19 Biddiss 3-49	RUASCC 168-7 Hallam 32, Roffey 30* Orme 20	Won by 3 wickets
22 Aug.	H	Checkendon 231-4 dec. Powell 122*	RUASCC 234-4 Avis 86*, Walden 60 Sewell 35, Amin 35*	Won by 6 wickets
25 Aug.	A	RUASCC 105 Sewell 30, Budd 23 Tranter 22	Whitchurch 106-7 Tranter 4-28 Ridley 3-43	Lost by 3 wickets

29 Aug.	H	RUASCC 178-8 dec. Tranter 53* Hotten 35, Walden 20	Reading 'A' 123-6 Pursglove 4-22	Drawn
1 Sept.	H	RUASCC 203-4 dec. Sewell 87, Amin 39 Budd 31, Hallam 20*	Stoke Row 192-8 Ridley 4-61	Drawn
4 Sept.	H	RUASCC 130 Budd 37, Fleming 31	Woodley 134-9	Lost by 1 wicket
5 Sept.	H	Eversley 180-3 dec.	RUASCC 183-7 Budd 96*, Roffey 23	Won by 3 wickets
8 Sept.	H	Farley Hill 176-5 dec.	RUASCC 138-7 Ansell 59, Sewell 44	Drawn
11 Sept.	H	RUASCC 97 Miles 22, Sewell 21	Warborough 98-1	Lost by 9 wickets
15 Sept.	A	Newbury 176-8 dec.	RUASCC 177-7 Ison 49, Sewell 31 Walden 29, Hallam 25	Won by 3 wickets
19 Sept.	H	Braywick 186-7 dec. Fitzgerald 4-42	RUASCC 104 Tranter 32* Hallam 20	Lost by 82 runs
23 Sept.	H	RUASCC 146-9 dec. Walden 56, Giles 40	N. I. R. D. 134 Orme 4-42	Won by 12 runs
25 Sept.	H	Reading Lawyers 176-8 dec. Tranter 3-44	RUASCC 139-8 Tranter 31, Ison 22 Hotten 20	Drawn

Some Club and individual records

Season by season summary of results.

Playing record against opponents.

Leading appearances.

Leading run-makers, and centuries.

Leading wicket-takers, and 7 or more wickets in an innings.

Century and record partnerships.

Single Wicket Tournament; Club Award.

Sir George Edwards Trophy.

Miscellaneous records.

Season by Season Summary of Results

	Played	Won	Lost	Drawn	Tied	% Won	% Undefeated
1964	14	7	5	2	0	50	64
1965	22	7	8	7	0	33	64
1966	20	4	10	6	0	20	50
1967	21	6	9	4	2	29	57
1968	17	7	8	2	0	41	53
1969	25	3	9	13	0	12	64
1970	20	5	6	9	0	25	70
1971	20	4	7	9	0	20	65
1972	26	4	6	16	0	15	77
1973	23	6	6	11	0	26	74
1974	29	10	10	8	1	34	66
1975	34	12	13	9	0	35	62
1976	39	13	16	10	0	33	59
1977	34	13	9	12	0	38	74
1978	42	18	11	12	1	43	74
1979	47	13	22	12	0	28	53
1980	52	20	9	23	0	38	83
1981	46	11	10	24	1	21	69
1982	50	15	15	20	0	30	70
Totals	581	178	189	209	5	31	67

Playing Record against opponents (79) since 1964

Clubs listed in chronological order of date first played. Dates in brackets indicate the year of first fixture if opponents were played before 1964, when score-books were not kept. Asterisk indicates opponents played in 1982.

(P = Played, W = Won, L = Lost, D = Drawn, T = Tied)

	P	W	L	D	T	% W	% L
1964							
R. U. Students' 2nd XI (1957)*	26	8	9	9	0	31	35
Reading Police*	8	3	3	2	0	38	38
Newbury Wednesday (1963)*	20	8	5	7	0	40	25
East Tytherley	4	0	2	2	0	0	50
Wokingham Wednesday and 3rd XI (1963)	17	3	9	5	0	18	53
R. U. Employees (1957)	22	14	3	5	0	64	14
S. M. S. Hermitage	19	6	10	3	0	32	53
The Particulars (1960)	4	1	2	1	0	25	50
Southampton University Academic Staff (1961)*	20	4	10	6	0	20	50
1965							
R. A. F. Shinfield	4	1	3	0	0	25	75
Staff College Owls*	15	6	6	3	0	40	40
Nautical Coll. Pangbourne Staff	3	0	0	2	1	0	0
R. U. Postgraduates/Casuals	3	2	0	1	0	67	0
R. U. Students' 1st XI*	18	1	9	8	0	6	50
Bristol University Academicals (1961)	10†	1	2	7	0	10	20
A. Harrison's XI	1	0	1	0	0	0	100
R. A. F. Benson	4	0	2	2	0	0	50

† Full record since 1961 — Played 13, Won 1, Lost 4, Drawn 8

	P	W	L	D	T	% W	% L
1966							
Wallingford	4	1	2	1	0	25	50
Leckford*	23	6	8	8	1	26	35
Leeds University Staff	2	2	0	0	0	100	0

163

	P	W	L	D	T	% W	% L
1967							
I. C. I. Bozedown House	2	1	0	0	1	50	0
1968							
Shiplake College Wanderers*	13	4	2	7	0	31	15
Cardiff University Staff (1962)	2	0	1	1	0	0	50
Hurstbourne Priors	2	1	1	0	0	50	50
1969							
Reading School All Stars*	19	4	9	6	0	21	47
Bradfield College	2	1	0	1	0	50	0
Abingdon*	15	4	5	6	0	27	33
Southampton College of Technology	1	0	0	1	0	0	0
Flamingo	1	0	0	1	0	0	0
1970							
Woodley*	9	2	3	4	0	22	33
1971							
Milton Keynes	3	1	2	0	0	33	67
University of Sussex Staff	6	0	2	4	0	0	33
St Margaretsbury	2	0	1	1	0	0	50
D. Robertson's XI	2	2	0	0	0	100	0
1972							
Surrey University Staff*	12	7	3	2	0	58	25
Bluecoat School*	10	5	2	3	0	50	20
L. S. E.	6	2	1	3	0	33	17
Caversham*	15	1	7	7	0	7	47
Cirencester	2	0	0	2	0	0	0
1973							
Royal Ascot*	17	3	5	9	0	18	29
Bearwood College Staff	1	0	0	1	0	0	0
Bramshill Police College*	14	3	4	7	0	21	29

	P	W	L	D	T	% W	% L
Mandarins*	19	9	4	6	0	47	21
Allen & Unwin	5	2	2	1	0	40	40
1974							
R. U. Students' 3rd XI	7	4	0	3	0	57	0
Green Park	6	4	1	1	0	67	17
Christchurch College	4	0	3	1	0	0	75
Reading Lawyers*	16	5	3	8	0	31	19
1975							
Checkendon*	14	5	5	4	0	36	36
Stoke Row*	10	2	1	6	1	20	10
1976							
Wokingham Schoolmasters*	5	3	2	0	0	60	40
West Ilsley	3	1	2	0	0	33	67
Mapledurham*	6	0	3	3	0	0	50
Hurst*	12	2	4	6	0	17	33
1977							
U. C. L.*	6	3	1	2	0	50	17
Exeter University Staff*	3	3	0	0	0	100	0
N. I. R. D.*	10	6	1	2	1	60	10
1978							
Leighton Park School*	5	3	1	1	0	60	20
Sonning	1	0	1	0	0	0	100
K. C. L.	1	1	0	0	0	100	0
Fairmile Hospital	1	0	1	0	0	0	100
Whitchurch (Hants)*	8	3	1	4	0	38	13
Reading A XI*	5	1	1	3	0	20	20
1979							
Nettlebed*	7	0	2	5	0	0	29
Shinfield*	4	0	1	3	0	0	25
Wellington Schoolmasters*	4	0	4	0	0	0	100

	P	W	L	D	T	% W	% L
Littlewick Green*	3	0	2	1	0	0	67
Savernake Forest	1	1	0	0	0	100	0
Tilehurst*	4	1	1	2	0	25	25
Gloucestershire Clergy	2	2	0	0	0	100	0
Hartley Wintney	1	0	1	0	0	0	100
Warborough*	4	2	2	0	0	50	50
Knowl Hill*	5	2	0	3	0	40	0

1980

	P	W	L	D	T	% W	% L
Farley Hill*	5	0	1	4	0	0	20
Finchampstead	1	0	1	0	0	0	100
Coley Park	1	1	0	0	0	100	0
Braywick*	5	2	2	1	0	40	40

1981

	P	W	L	D	T	% W	% L
Merry Mowers*	2	1	1	0	0	50	50
Eversley*	2	1	0	1	0	50	0

1982

No new fixtures

Leading appearances 1964-1982 (qualification: 100)

M. J. Sewell	339 in 15 seasons
A. K. Giles	320 in 19 seasons
D. J. Ansell	299 in 16 seasons
R. D. Pearce	279 in 14 seasons
W. D. Redfern	240 in 18 seasons
R. J. Loader	237 in 12 seasons
J. R. Knowlson	237 in 13 seasons
D. M. Pursglove	225 in 9 seasons
R. B. Tranter	193 in 8 seasons
D. H. Robertson	155 in 8 seasons
P. Fitzgerald	140 in 7 seasons
M. D. S. Butler	132 in 7 seasons
D. J. Petherick	126 in 4 seasons
G. R. Crampton	123 in 6 seasons
G. E. Dalton	117 in 7 seasons
R. W. Willey	102 in 8 seasons
K. Robinson	100 in 12 seasons

'Seasons' are those during which players were ordinarily available

Leading run-makers 1964-1982
(qualification: 1000 runs and average of 15)

	Runs	Innings	N. O.	H. Score	Av.
M. J. Sewell	9101	334	53	113*	32.4
D. J. Ansell	5293	275	17	103*	20.5
J. R. Knowlson	4507	215	44	111*	26.4
A. K. Giles	4488	289	51	85	18.9
M. D. S. Butler	4109	127	23	156*	39.5
D. H. Robertson	3343	153	17	98*	24.6
R. J. Loader	2904	216	25	82	15.2
G. E. Dalton	2553	106	12	97	27.2
R. B. Tranter	2247	149	42	73*	21.0
M. R. Avis	1695	58	15	112*	39.4
G. R. Crampton	1481	109	11	86	15.1
A. Harrison	1408	92	6	84	16.4
R. Ison	1145	48	1	91	24.4

Centuries

M. R. Heslehurst	124	v.	Mandarins	1975	
J. Humberstone	101	v.	Allen & Unwin	1975	
D. J. Ansell	102	v.	Allen & Unwin	1976	
J. R. Knowlson	111*	v.	Green Park	1978)	within
M. D. S. Butler	117*	v.	Bluecoat School	1978)	6 days
M. J. Sewell	113*	v.	Shiplake College Wand.	1978)	
M. J. Sewell	101*	v.	Leighton Park School	1979	
M. D. S. Butler	100*	v.	Employees	1979	
M. D. S. Butler	101*	v.	Caversham	1979	
P. R. Crane	101*	v.	Caversham	1979	
M. D. S. Butler	114*	v.	Warborough	1979	
M. R. Avis	112*	v.	Surrey Univ. Staff	1980	
M. D. S. Butler	104*	v.	Nettlebed	1980	
D. J. Ansell	103*	v.	Coley Park	1980	
M. D. S. Butler	101*	v.	Students' 2nd XI	1982	
M. D. S. Butler	156*	v.	Newbury	1982	

* not out

Leading wicket-takers 1964-1982 (qualification: 100)

	Wkts	Overs	Mdns	Runs	Av.
R. B. Tranter	325	1719	306	5850	18.0
A. K. Giles	269	1157	113	4829	17.9
D. J. Petherick	265	1362	276	4261	16.1
M. D. Pursglove	262	1186	104	5135	19.6
K. Robinson	221	1101	198	3414	15.4
P. Fitzgerald	203	804	56	4309	21.2
G. E. Dalton	194	1029	158	3394	17.5
R. W. Willey	187	914	194	2591	13.9
D. J. Ansell	147	949	116	3637	24.7
W. D. Redfern	104	569	76	1971	19.0

7 or more wickets in an innings

A. Harrison	7-24	v.	Newbury	1965
R. W. Willey	7-11	v.	Employees	1965
J. E. Flower	8-29	v.	S. M. S. Hermitage	1967
K. Robinson	8-48	v.	Newbury	1970
C. R. C. Hendy	8-33	v.	S. M. S. Hermitage	1974
A. K. Giles	8-43	v.	Surrey Univ. Staff	1975
C. Nixon	7-33	v.	Reading Lawyers	1976
R. B. Tranter	7-44	v.	N. I. R. D.	1977
P. Fitzgerald	7-29	v.	Green Park	1978
G. Norman	7-29	v.	Royal Ascot	1978
R. Smith	9-28	v.	Reading Lawyers	1978
D. J. Petherick	7-62	v.	Whitchurch	1978
A. G. Robiette	8-29	v.	S. M. S. Hermitage	1978
D. J. Petherick	8-20	v.	U. C. L.	1980
M. D. Pursglove	8-31	v.	Students' 3rd XI	1980
J. A. Gartner	7-35	v.	Employees	1980
J. S. Elder	7-37	v.	Checkendon	1981

Century and record partnerships 1964-1982

Score	Batsmen		Opponents	Venue	Date
1st Wicket					
232†	M. D. S. Butler	156*	Newbury	H	1/5/82
	M. J. Sewell	60*			
186†	M. J. Sewell	58*	Warborough	H	8/9/79
	M. D. S. Butler	114*			
167	D. J. Ansell	70	Bristol University		
	G. E. Dalton	92	Academicals	A	15/7/68
154	M. J. Sewell	89	Students' 1st XI	H	4/5/80
	J. R. Knowlson	72			
152†	D. J. Ansell	103*	Coley Park	H	6/9/80
	P. Hotten	27*			
140	J. R. Knowlson	49*	David		
	G. E. Dalton	88	Robertson's XI	H	16/7/72
134†	M. R. Avis	66*	Shiplake College		
	M. J. Sewell	52*	Wanderers	A	20/5/82
134	M. J. Sewell	66*	Allen & Unwin	H	25/6/77
	J. R. Knowlson	63			
131	M. J. Sewell	64	Reading Lawyers	H	28/6/75
	M. R. Heslehurst	66			
122	M. J. Sewell	86*	Shiplake College		
	R. J. Loader	37	Wanderers	A	26/5/77
121	R. J. Loader	56	Green Park	H	15/5/76
	R. Thomas	70			
116	D. J. Ansell	85	Leckford	H	27/6/70
	M. J. Sewell	30			
113	J. R. Knowlson	50	Reading Lawyers	H	29/6/74
	M. J. Sewell	65			
113	M. J. Sewell	61	Surrey University		
	R. J. Loader	82	Staff	A	4/6/78
112	G. E. Dalton	85	Sussex University		
	R. J. Loader	34	Staff	H	23/7/72
111	M. J. Sewell	64	Hurst	H	19/4/81
	M. D. S. Butler	53			
106	M. J. Sewell	53	Wokingham	A	12/5/76
	R. J. Loader	67			

170

Score	Batsmen		Opponents	Venue	Date
102	R. J. Loader	23	Cardiff University		
	D. J. Ansell	74	Staff	H	12/7/69
101	M. J. Sewell	60	Caversham	H	24/4/76
	R. J. Loader	28			

2nd Wicket

214†	P. R. Crane	101*	Caversham	A	22/7/79
	M. D. S. Butler	101*			
157	M. R. Heslehurst	124*	Mandarins	H	13/7/75
	G. E. Dalton	54			
137	M. J. Sewell	53	Exeter Erratics	A	15/7/81
	M. D. S. Butler	85			
133	M. R. Avis	112*	Surrey University	A	1/6/80
	R. Ison	64	Staff	A	1/6/80
118	G. E. Dalton	67*	Newbury	H	3/7/68
	D. Robertson	41			
118	M. J. Sewell	70*	Checkendon	H	28/8/77
	M. D. S. Butler	64			
117†	M. D. S. Butler	70*	Mandarins	H	12/7/81
	J. R. Knowlson	63*			
117	D. J. Ansell	69	Woodley	H	23/7/75
	G. E. Dalton	55			
112	M. D. S. Butler	73	Reading A XI	H	3/9/78
	S. W. Adkins	65			
105	M. J. Sewell	80	Staff College		
	M. D. S. Butler	89*	Owls	A	28/6/81
100	M. J. Sewell	37	Braywick	H	20/9/81
	M. D. S. Butler	62			

3rd Wicket

120	C. H. Walker	85	David		
	M. R. Heslehurst	48*	Robertson's XI	H	11/7/71
112	J. Budd	83	Mandarins	H	11/7/82
	P. Hotten	33			
108	M. J. Sewell	52	Allen & Unwin	H	12/6/76
	D. J. Ansell	102			
104†	M. J. Sewell	101*	Leighton Park		
	J. A. Gartner	49*	School	H	23/6/79
103	J. Benton	51*	Whitchurch	H	30/8/78
	D. J. Ansell	58			
103	M. R. Avis	112*	Surrey University		
	G. Norman	57	Staff	A	1/6/80

171

Score	Batsmen		Opponents	Venue	Date
4th Wicket					
126	J. R. Knowlson	67	Surrey University		
	M. D. S. Butler	75	Staff	H	1/6/75
105	D. J. Ansell	56	Southampton Coll.		
	D. Robertson	73	of Technology	A	8/7/69
5th Wicket					
145†	M. D. S. Butler	100*	Employees	H	7/7/79
	M. J. Sewell	55*			
102	J. R. Knowlson	76	Southampton Univ.		
	A. K. Giles	37	Academic Staff	H	11/6/78
100†	D. J. Ansell	71*	Reading Lawyers	H	7/7/76
	D. G. Hay	29*			
6th Wicket					
82†	M. R. Heslehurst	48*	Abingdon	H	22/7/71
	R. W. Willey	48*			
82	M. D. Biddiss	43	Bramshill Police		
	R. D. Pearce	35	College	H	21/4/82
7th Wicket					
99	J. K. Dugdale	26	Reading Police	H	13/7/66
	R. W. Willey	60			
8th Wicket					
63	R. Ison	75	Tilehurst	H	13/6/82
	R. B. Tranter	30*			
9th Wicket					
48	B. Loughborough	20*	Southampton Univ.		
	F. Robertson	14	Academic Staff	H	6/7/65
10th Wicket					
51	D. R. Thomas	47*	Ian Fletcher's		
	I. P. Williams	8	Particulars	H	3/7/65

† unbroken
* not out

172

Finals of the Single Wicket Tournament

1965	K. Robinson	beat	A. Harrison
1966	A. K. Giles	beat	W. D. Redfern
1967	B. D. Dore	beat	S. D. Smith
1968	D. J. Ansell	beat	A. Harrison
1969	R. D. Pearce	beat	D. J. Ansell
1970	M. R. Heslehurst	beat	R. D. Pearce
1971	M. R. Heslehurst	beat	R. W. Willey
1972	not played		
1973*	G. E. Dàlton	beat	R. W. Willey
1974*	C. H. Walker	beat	R. W. Willey
1975	not played		
1976*	D. J. Ansell	beat	D. Edwards

* 'Bill & Babs Cup' held by winner for one year

Recipients of the Club Award

1979	M. J. Sewell
1980	M. D. S. Butler
1981	M. J. Sewell
1982	P. Fitzgerald

Sir George Edwards' Trophy

	Winners	Runners up	Third	Wooden spoon	Venue
1975	Surrey	L. S. E.	So'ton	Reading	Guildford
1976	Surrey	Reading	So'ton	L. S. E.	Reading
1977	Surrey	So'ton	Reading	Exeter	Southampton
1978	Reading	So'ton	K. C. L.	Surrey	Guildford
1979	Reading	Surrey	Exter	So'ton	Reading
1980	Exeter	So'ton	Reading	Surrey	Exeter
1981	So'ton	Reading	Exeter	Surrey	So'ton

1982   Rain on the second day prevented a final being played. On the first day, Reading beat Exeter and Surrey beat So'ton. The venue was Reading.

174

Miscellaneous records

Most appearances in a season — 40, M. J. Sewell, 1982

Most runs in a season — 1,439, M. J. Sewell, 1982

Highest ever individual score — 156*, M. D. S. Butler, v. Newbury, 1982

Most wickets in a season — 66, D. J. Petherick, 1979

Best ever analysis — 9-28, R. Smith, v. Reading Lawyers, 1978

Most catches in a season — 26, P. R. Crane, 1978

Highest score by RUASCC — 259 for 7, v. Exeter University Erratics, 1981

Highest score against RUASCC — 247 for 4, v. Reading School All Stars, 1981

Lowest score by RUASCC — 25, v. Milton Keynes, 1971

Lowest score against RUASCC — 41, v. Caversham, 1976

Most matches played in a season — 52, 1980

Most wins in a season — 20, 1980

Highest percentage of wins in a season — 50, 1964

Highest percentage of undefeated games — 83, 1980

Most years as captain — 6, D. J. Ansell, 1972-5, 1982-3

Most frequently played opponents (outside the University) — Leckford, 23

Players completing the 'double' of 1000 runs and 100 wickets

D. J. Ansell*	5293 runs and 147 wickets in 16 seasons
G. E. Dalton	2553 runs and 194 wickets in 7 seasons
A. K. Giles*	4488 runs and 269 wickets in 19 seasons
W. D. Redfern	2086 runs and 104 wickets in 18 seasons
R. B. Tranter	2247 runs and 325 wickets in 8 seasons

* These players have also been amongst the Club's regular wicket keepers

A gallery of sporting prints

Being the catalogue of an exhibition at the Museum of English Rural Life celebrating the Golden Jubilee of the Reading University Academic Staff Cricket Club, Summer 2004.

Cyril Tyler hanging up his boots

The Academic Staff 1st XI Ground, Elmhurst Road

Harrison counts the opposition

The Old Changing Shed, 1938-1978

Syd in mid-stream at Bristol

A moth drops into Fred's supper at Marlborough

Des Smith hooks to fine leg: shirt out, cap off

Fletcher at mid-on in braces and brogues

Redfern puts out a fag

Osborne comments on the beer

David Ansell completing an on-drive

Keither Robinson gets a hand to one in the slips

The Electric Storm at Southampton, c. 1970

A. K. Giles pacing out his run-up

Robert Pearce taking grip

A sextet of fast bowlers:

     Chris Evans lets one go

     Dore fails to let go

     Carey Hendy training in the sheep field

     Bob Willey delivering a yorker

     David Petherick delivering piglets

     Graham Dalton delivering a sermon

Dalton's onslaught before preaching

Robinson and Giles discuss the field — 45 yards apart!

Roger Loader catches it in the gully

007 Fitzgerald bowls from behind dark glasses

Foot blocks one at short square leg

Dalton's cap

The bald ones replace the grey ones

The New Changing Shed, 1978-2004

Light and Darkness in a Knowlson Innings
A sequence of steel engravings reproduced, by gracious permission of the Editor, from the *Journal of Beckett Studies* for the year 1984:

    James Knowlson taking a single

    James Knowlson striking the ball to short mid-wicket

    James Knowlson occupying the crease

    Knowlson's six

Holes in the netting

Dobbs advises Giles on his field placing

Sewell and Ansell debating a single

David Ansell turning for the fourth run

Same player chases one to fine leg at Leckford

David Robertson taking guard (two)

Peter Crane plays forward watchfully, bat angled

Angela Redfern's tea

Mike Sewell adjusting the field

Seismographic readings recorded as A. K. Giles takes a diving catch at mid-on

Set of three engraved plates, courtesy 'Mathematics at Play':

    Sewell takes his bat away, c. 1968

    Sewell middles same ball, c. 1974

    Sewell hits same ball for four, c. 1978

An inscribed copy 'Catastrophe Theory and Cricket Tactics' by M. J. Sewell

George Norman thanks captain for taking him off

George Norman apologises to captain for thanking him for taking him off

Caistor bowls to Cirencester opening batsman. Score 210 for 0

A cultural evening out in Bristol

Loader flashes outside the off stump

Robiette unplayable at Hermitage

Sewell and Robertson at breakfast

Pursglove bowls Gibson of Surrey with his googly

Colin Walker receives 'best dressed player of the year' award

Colin Walker arrives for 2.30 pm start. Photograph dated 14.7.72, 3 pm

The old scoring hut and board, c. 1970, and the New electronic scoreboard, 2001

Baum bats in yellow socks

The Rev. 'lifted' on to the railway line at Wokingham

Dr W. D. Redfern addressing the ball

George Norman addressing the umpire

Tranter and Crane winning the Trophy

St George Edwards addresses Joe Pais

Colonials:

> Max Heslehurst telephoning his woman
>
> Roger Smith calling off the lawyers
>
> Joe Gartner getting acclimatised
>
> Alan Rugman finds 'the going hard' at Ascot

Butler's drive

Dai Edwards at work in the covers

Grey hounds standing in the slips

Giles bowls his 24-yarder

The umpire addressing George Norman

Loader receives a winged Messenger

The Former Captain's XI, 1990

Dr R. W. Willey produces a crop of wickets

Fred Robertson gives a decision

Crampton receives the call to arms early on Sunday morning

Avis returns one to Loader

Loader getting up

The Treasurer counting the contents of his Box

Alan Harrison declares after tea

A quintet of slow bowlers:

>Pursglove manages to pitch his googly

>Giles' straight one

>Fitzgerald spearheads the attack against Surrey

>Knowlson getting bounce

>Sewell opens the bowling against Sussex

M. D. S. Butler with cricket bag (courtesy of Sainsburys)

Wild Scenes at The Nob

The Leckford Hut

The Old Bath, demolished c. 1978

The filming of Colin Walker's action

Baggageman moving into position at mid-on

Ansell, caught and bowled N. I. R. D. 0

Ridley's flannels

The Dean Elect's charge to the wicket

Orme goes fishing

Elder directing his field

Budd in full flow

Avis thinking them out

Ison safe, inside the boundary

Fitzgerald, going for the hat-trick after 8 months

Tranter doing some contra-accounting

Crampton catches one in the gully

Pearce is brought in to forward short leg

Walker arrives on time

Butler gets his jock strap in a twist

Wieczorek doing the Gydansk glide

Pursglove blames his shoulder

Knowlson, struck on the finger, apologises to the bowler

Hotten snaps one

Sewell studying the 1981 score book

Some famous grounds:

> The Long Room, Hermitage
>
> The Prairies, LSE
>
> The back of the pavilion, Checkendon
>
> The wicket, Green Park
>
> The Grandstand, Ascot
>
> The Bar, Bramshill
>
> Tranter's Tree, NIRD

Some famous opponents:

> Ron Austin digs in
>
> Eric Russell holes out to Robeson
>
> Darwin Crawford bowls out of the black sightscreen
>
> Crabtree throws his cap on the ground and jumps on it

The Pavilion Restaurant, 1995

Kerry Packer pleads with the Sports Facilities Committee

The Academic Staff arrive to tour Barbados, 1987

The Curators acknowledge the loan of valuable items from the collections of players of the Golden Age, which has made this exhibition possible.

	May			
	2	Students 2nd XI	H	2.30
R. Police	6	~~Owls C C Minley Manor~~	A	2.00	canc
	13	Newbury	A	2.30
	20	East Tytherley	A	2.00
	27	Wokingham	A	2.30

	June			
	1	~~Nautical College Staff~~	H		canc.
	3	R A F Shinfield	A	2.30
	4	Employees	H	6.30
2nd XI. Sat.	10	~~Bristol Staff~~	H		canc.

	June			
	16	School of Military Survey	A	6.00
	18	~~Students 2nd XI~~	H	5.00	canc.
	24	Newbury	H	2.30
	27	Particulars	H	2.30

	July			
	1	Particulars	A	2.30
	7	Southampton Staff	A	
	9	Employees	A	6.30
	15	Reading Police	H	2.30

The first fixture card, 1964

Index

Because of the frequency with which the names of opposing clubs and individual RUASCC players appear in the season by season reports, it has been felt impracticable and unnecessary to include them in this index. The names of a few pioneer members and personalities have, however, been included, together with certain places, events and achievements which have been important in the life of the Club.